Edward's
Xlibris Best

Edward's Xlibris Best

EDWARD R. LEVENSON, EDITOR

To order additional copies of this book, contact:
Xlibris
844-714-8691
www.Xlibris.com
Orders@Xlibris.com
784018

Preface

Dear readers, you can be happy for two reasons. First of all, you're looking at a "pretty good book." Secondly, as thc title reflects, I'm finally getting over my difficulties of my early youth in my family of having been "Edward-and-Only-Edward" and am gaining a new comfort as a senior with my first name. That is, in certain settings. Such as here, in *Edward's Xlibris Best.*

This, my eighth Xlibris book, needs no explanation. It is a selection of what I consider are my best pieces in my previous seven Xlibris books, which are:

"Edward's Humor" and More (February 2017),
Genres Mélange (October 2017),
Genres Mélange Deuxième (July 2018),
The View From Kings Point: The Kings Point [Creative]*
Writers Club Anthology, 2018 (September 2018) [*I mistakenly omitted the word *"Creative"* from the subtitle.],
Genres Synch (January 2019),
Epithalamium of Prose, Poetry, and Puzzles for Aliza and Yhali, December 29, 2019 (December 2019),
The View From Kings Point: The Kings Point Creative Writers Club Anthology, 2020 (December 2020).

My acronyms for the seven books are, in turn, *EHAM, GM, GMD, VKP, GS, E3PAY,* and *VKP2.* My acronym for *Edward's Xlibris Best* is *EXB.*

Three of the above books are anthologies; the other four are multi-genres mixes. The genres featured from all six books in this collection are "Humor," "Word Play" (actually a quasi-genre), "Poetry," "Fiction," "Memoirs," and "Interpretation." The last of the six terms listed, which I have used hitherto, should be understood as including "Reviews." Each of the six genres is represented by eight pieces. Eleven pieces among the 58 in the book were written by guest contributors, and they are noted as such with asterisks in the Table of Contents. Following the first six sections according to genre is a "mélange" of eight pieces culled exclusively from *VKP2* and a puzzle from *E3PAY* as well. Two special pieces are new. The word "*mélange*," to be sure, gives me good vibes because four of my books, as I mentioned, are multi-genres mixes; two of them, in fact, feature the word in their titles.

That the 58 pieces I have selected are "my best" is, of course, a subjective personal judgment. Xlibris, I feel sure, will welcome "fan mail" indicating readers' different preferences. That having been said, I recommend the last piece in *VKP2* and *EXB,* written jointly by Allan Korn and Yours Truly, "Who Says We're Not What We Say We Are?"

Of all my Xlibris cover designs, readers will undoubtedly agree that the one for *EXB* is the biggest "winner" of all because it includes all seven previous ones in an arrangement above and below the title and the list of the books.

I dedicate this book to all nine of my guest contributors, especially to my wife Reva–"the love of my life" (who has a "three-peat" by sheer coincidence, of course)–but no invidious comparisons must be drawn among the other eight loved ones and dear friends. The influence of one "contributor" not reflected explicitly in the writings is present everywhere in the book. I refer to my extraordinarily capable therapist, Dr. Marshall Fenster, a man of as much modesty, common sense, caring, and nobility of soul as he is of psychological expertise.

This collection, God willing, will be appearing in April 2021, a time fraught with anxiety over the worldwide Coronavirus pandemic. If it will afford a modicum of relief, diversion, enjoyment, and stimulation during the rigors of the "social distancing" and quarantining, I will be more grateful to you, my readers, for my being able to provide benefit to you than you will be to me. Be safe one and all!

March 8, 2021. I have added two late-edition sonnets in honor of much-esteemed helpers in the progress of the book.

Table of Contents

(Guest contributors are signified by asterisks.)

Poetry

Fiction

Memoirs

Interpretation/Reviews

Mélange

Thanks to Sheila Legaspi: a Sonnet[1]

She's not a Being in Heaven and hence transcendent
Like Muses of mine[2] that number over four
Though "*Caelum*" serves her as a worthy precedent[3]
The Hindi "*Sheela*"[4] and the Hebrew "*She'elah*"[5] are two more.

A new Production Manager for my books
The twenty-author anthology prodigious to complete[6]

---

[1] This poem may be viewed as complementary to my "Ode to Xlibris" (see page 143). Whereas the emotion in that one refers to my gratitude to the Company for the publication of many of my books over four years, this refers to my gratitude to one manager who stayed the course with me through severe production stresses during the much shorter period of four weeks.

[2] For example, Thea Aeide (see pages 144f.). Also, Erin McKean, CEO of Wordnik, who wrote me on March 7th, "I'd be very flattered to be included in your list of Muses."

[3] Wikipedia, "Sheila" and "Celia"; and assorted popular internet websites. An antecedent name of "Sheila" is said to be "Celia," a derivative of the Latin "*Caelius*," signifying belonging to the distinguished Roman Caelius family. The meaning of the family name was "heavenly," "*caelum*" having meant "sky" or "heavens," as in the English "celestial." I thus could have considered Sheila as being transcendent on the basis of the name; but our relationship involved intense practical tasks, not inspiration. With my wife Reva it is both, but in her case too, there is sufficient "this side" interaction that Reva is not a Muse for me either, just sometimes. Another antecedent name of Sheila may be the Gaelic "*caol*," which means "straight and narrow," as referring either to a body of water or an isthmus of land. The masculine name "Kyle" may be a derivative of that.

[4] Wikipedia, "Sheela." The name in Hindi/Sanskrit means "character, good conduct."

[5] This is an original association of Yours Truly. "*She'elah*" (pronounced "sh'aylah") means a "question" in Hebrew. The word has particular relevance and resonance for me in connection with Sheila because of her many queries to me in clarification of corrections I requested in the finalization of the manuscripts of the two books she managed.

[6] *The View From Kings Point: The Kings Point Creative Writers Club Anthology, 2020.*

Edward's Xlibris Best how glorious it looks!
Overview of four full years my joy's replete!

Legaspi got me to the long-sought goal
Evoked my audible gasp, "We finally gained it!"
More books to come I'm not so very ole.[7]
Grief's past. On tap's new sharpening of my wit.

"Asot s'farim harbeh eyn kets."[8] Tremendous!
The help of wondrous Sheila has been stupendous!

---

[7] At least I hope not.

[8] The Hebrew original for "Of making many books there is no end" (Ecclesiastes 12:12). I quoted this verse in my volta to my "Ode to Xlibris" (see the first note above and page 143).

AUM and *EXB*

For Murji, Anjni, Eli, and Kishor,
Thanks from the heart for all you've done for me.
Not to forget Keilyne she's now one more.
The best of Edward's done. Acronymed it's *EXB*.

An unknown entity the "X" is not.
The Latin preposition "*ex*" it means,
"Out of the books"—of eight I now have wrought,
Fulfillment of five years of fruitful dreams.

A "Plate of Book" you'll find inside in "Humor,"
For books in others' libraries not just in mine.
"AUM" in "Word Play" follows shortly after,
My trusted friends and helpers in this troubled time.

We pray the dreaded virus will reach its limits
And more Xlibris books will lift our spirits.

HUMOR

Possession, Certificate of, and Plate of Book

Ex Libris

Excellentibus, Stupendis, et Admirandis*

(from the excellent, stupendous, and

SIMPLY-MUST-BE-ADMIRED* books) of:

_____

This **Epithalamium** copy–whether pawned off or presented to; or pocketed, purchased, or purloined by

_____

is an original "wedding favor" created for the occasion of the blessed wedding on December 29, 2019 of

Aliza and Yhali

with heartfelt hopes for everything heartfelt hopes are wished. Offered with deep love and respect for all.

Proudísimo (Orgullosísimo) Pater of the 38+
personae, *Abba* and *Papá Abba* Levenson

*Aliza–and brothers Judah and Benjamin–will confirm that the Latin gerundive of obligation *NON FUDGENDUM EST* (no invidious allusion to Atlantic City toffee intended)!

Prayer, sort of (Playful)
of Stepmom Reva

ALIZA AND YHALI UNITE
by Stepmom Reva Luxenberg Levenson

Two lovely young women
I now introduce
At this festive occasion
As you can deduce.

In the City of Brotherly Love
Aliza and Yhali will join
We throw in the fountain
For good luck many a coin.

Meeting in Mexico
Was a stroke of good luck
Gravitating together
With love were awestruck.

The music played softly
Aliza was altruistic
When they both danced
Yhali so optimistic.

They clung together
And did verify
That one happy day
They would unify.

Now here's a celebration
With love an overview

Of a gathering of folks
Making a hullabaloo.

I speak from my heart
With this certitude
That they both will grow
With a loving magnitude.

I wish them a good life
Behind a closed door
Peace and good health
And loads of *amor*.

On Humor in the *Tanakh* (Hebrew Scriptures),

by Rabbi Sylvan Kamens

My teacher Dr. Mordecai Kaplan of blessed memory was often quoted as saying that there is no humor in the *Tanakh*. While it is true that there is little of "funny ha-ha" or out-loud laughing, there are a number of events that are filled with irony, satire, and sarcasm. Rabbi Milton Steinberg wrote a little book more than 60 years ago called *Certain People of the Book*. A few examples from this book will make my point.

We are all familiar with the Jacob and Esau scene in Genesis in which the starving hunter returns to the encampment. We are supposed to believe that nowhere in the entire neighborhood is there any other food save the lentil stew that Jacob has whipped up. "Give me of that red, red stuff," cries the hungry hunter in anguish. Then Jacob seizes the moment and sells it to him for his birthright. We chuckle, for it makes of Esau a buffoon, rather than a man of equal stature with his brother.

We read in Numbers of King Balak, who buys the services of the leading shaman of the day, Balaam, to place curses upon the people of Israel. They proceed to go up and down mountains seeking the right place from which Balaam could hurl down his invective. But when all is said and done, Balaam rises up and delivers blessings upon the enemy. What we are left with is Balak, in effect, channeling Laurel and Hardy, saying "What a fine mess you've gotten me into!"

We have a description in First Samuel of God's commandment to Saul to eradicate the Amalekites, man and beast. Saul, who has just returned from battle, spares King Agag and some of the animals to use them for sacrifices. When Samuel comes upon Saul, the king is looking for approval from the prophet. Samuel asks, *"Meh qol hatzon?"* (What is this [bleating] sound of the sheep?) The use of "*Meh*" here is a very humorous onomatopoeia.

Perhaps the funniest book in the Bible is the Book of Esther. We have a snarling villain (Haman), a silly king (Ahasuaerus), a brave maiden (Esther), and a hero with a white hat to the rescue (Mordechai). The banquet scene is something out of the silent movie *The Perils of Pauline."*

While it is true that the *Tanakh* is an anthology of the most serious literature, these examples show that the Bible does make room for laughter.

It's Time for Me to Start Wearing My Hearing Aid, II

Last year I wrote a piece about my not wearing my hearing aid. Recently, in truth, I have been wearing it more–when it is absolutely necessary. For example, when Reva and I watch Agatha Christie mysteries with Hercule Poirot (played by David Sucher), I don't wear it–because his have subtitles; but I do wear it watching the mysteries with Jane Marple (played by Geraldine McEwan)–because hers don't. To be sure, I can hear speech, but often I don't hear the right words. Sometimes I irritate Reva when I mis-hear what she has said; but, as was the case last year, a number of my mistakes are very humorous indeed. Here is a new batch:

I needed to indicate to Reva that I would need a few minutes before coming to dinner because I had "to go to the bathroom," and she replied, "You're allowed!"
I thought she said, "Not too loud!"

Once Reva pointed out, "You have shaving cream under your ear!" I thought she said, "There's a tear in the seam of your rear!"

At the beginning of July I had a check to mail to the Woodbridge Cemetery for my new pre-need grave next to Reva's (after we reach 120–God willing). Reva had been watching a report on TV about the President's trouble with the IRS about concealing income and exclaimed, "Trump has not been declaring emoluments!"
I replied, "Did you just say I can't die until I pay all my installments?!"

Just like last year she asked me to buy at Publix six red potatoes, and I bought six red tomatoes. She said, "Next time get six red potatoes *and* six red tomatoes!"

Last year I mistook "Keep calm" for "Lower your arm" (I would register "ahm" in Bostonese, but I still thought Reva said "cahm").

This year I mistakenly heard "There's no hahm" for "I don't want to go to West Palm."

I had a cough, and Reva, from the living room, said, "tea with honey is my suggestion!"
I was in the kitchen and thought she said, "Take Robitussin for your congestion!"

She gave me the coordinates of a restaurant as "Jog and Glades." I thought she said, "Thank God for hearing aids."
And I replied, "I know I need to wear my hearing aid more."

Reva finished a phone conversation, and I asked, "Who called?"
She replied, "It was the druggist."
I thought she said, "It was your brother."
My hearing must be getting worse. That wasn't even close.

My Bookcase Dream

April 2017. On the Intermediate Sabbath of Passover Week, the Torah reading (Exodus 33:12–34:26) was about Moses' ascent of Mount Sinai to receive the Ten Commandments for the second time.

Early in the morning of the Eighth Day of Passover this year I had one of my most remarkable dreams ever. I dreamt that our rabbi–Rabbi Raphael Adler of Temple Anshei Shalom in Delray Beach, Florida– was descending the mountain, not with engraved stone tablets, but with a wooden Fresh Finds, Inc. bookcase. I mentioned the dream to *Rebbetsin* Francine Adler in synagogue some hours later; and she replied, "Let me get this straight. The rabbi was carrying a bookcase, but no books! Is that right?"

I recognized on the spot that the *rebbetsin* had an insight that had eluded me: the bookcase was the divinely inspired symbol of the *ordering* of divine wisdom, which was as important, unthinkable as this might seem, as the wisdom itself. To be sure, a major Passover symbol is "*seder*," which means "order"; and the Passover songs at the conclusion of the *Seder* service in the *Haggadah*–"*Eḥad Mi Yode'a*" (Who Knows One) and "*Ḥad Gadya*" (The Only Kid)–embody the numerical *ordering* of sacred symbols in Judaism and a chronological pecking *order* and downfall of the enemies of the Jewish people, respectively. The main function of the bookcase symbol in the dream was that divine wisdom–mythological, as well as historical–needs to be put into some kind of order.

In my personal context, I am presently structuring two projects: first, the rearrangement of my study and, second, my next book. For the former, I have bought bookcases online from a company called "Fresh Finds, Inc." One of those bookcases, obviously, got featured in the dream. The bookcases are, indeed, "finds," evoking in my mind the Hebrew and Yiddish word "*m'tsiah*" (a find), meaning more than just "luck," but "wonder," and even "miracle." The bookcases, which unfold when removed from the boxes, are marvels of construction. Rabbi Adler wasn't just lucky to find a Fresh Finds bookcase on top of Mount Sinai; God made a special presentation of it to him.

And why? The answer, I think, is found in the *"Eḥad Mi Yode'a"* song–in the numberings. "Who knows *five? Five* are the Five Books of Moses." "Who knows *six? Six* are the Six Orders of the *Mishnah"* (the basis of the Talmud). *Four* and *Nine* (the Four Matriarchs and the Nine Months of Childbirth) represent the increasing recognition of the importance in Judaism of "Women's Wisdom." *Ten* is the Ten Commandments. *Thirteen* are the Thirteen Attributes of God's Compassion.

Interestingly, Rabbi Adler, in the dream, was bringing down from the mountain a personal bookcase for *me.* After all, tradition holds that Jews of all generations were individually present at the bottom. The bookcase thus symbolizes that *my* creativity–however quirky and far out it might be–links me to the Jewish people and the Jewish tradition, as well as to the cultures and wisdom of the world.

My book *"Edward's Humor" and More* has five sections: "Humor," "Word Play," "Personae," "Memoirs," and "Interpretation." For my next book, I anticipate adding two new sections: "Sonnets" and "Fiction." I want to put "My Bookcase Dream" into the "Humor" section. If "My Colonoscopy" and "My New Grave" could fit into the "Humor" section of my first book, surely "My Bookcase Dream" can fit into that of the next one. But it is serious also.

Haggadah	Hebrew. "the booklet of the Passover *Seder* ritual"
rebbetsin, Rebbetsin	Hebrew. "rabbi's wife," "Rabbi's wife"

My Colonoscopy:
"Where the Sun Doesn't Shine"

In the 1975 film *The Sunshine Boys,* two cantankerous veteran comedians, Al Lewis and Willy Clark–played by George Burns and Walter Matthau–seek to come out of retirement and revive their partnership, which they had called Lewis and Clark: the Sunshine Boys. Clark (Matthau) was characteristically obstreperous in rejecting what he thought was not funny. He refused to do a commercial for a cereal called "Frumpies," because he felt that the word was uncomical since it had unsuitable consonants. "If it was funny, I'd say it. Like 'Alka-Seltzer', 'cupcake,' 'pickles,' 'chicken'–words with the 'k' sound. You don't get laughs with 'tomatoes' or 'lettuce'–or 'Frumpies.'"

Well, "colonoscopy" has *two* "k" sounds, though one fewer than "cupcake," which has three. And it is associated with "rectum," which has a "k" sound as well.

I offer that the location of the scope's probe represents an element of humor also. My wife Reva, God bless her, as a case in point, asked her gastroenterologist at the beginning of a colonoscopy procedure for her, "Does your mother know what you do for a living?"

Colonoscopy humor undeniably masks anxiety. I have a "redundant colon." It has loops, and doctors have difficulty getting through them. Three years ago I had a polyp as far inside as possible. Polyps are now described as "pre-cancerous" and are removed. My Philadelphia gastroenterologist was able to see mine with his scope, but he felt he couldn't remove it safely with the snare connected to it because it was too difficult to reach. He referred me to a colorectal surgeon, who, with an associate, accessed it through two incisions in my abdomen and one monitor through the rear entrance. The surgeon afterwards told me that the operation, which took several hours, was the most difficult "successful procedure" of his entire career.

Colonoscopy preparation is a subject in itself. The digestive tract must be completely cleaned out. For five days preceding, iron must not be consumed. On the day before the procedure, one must imbibe only clear liquids, as well as four Dulcolax pills, plus 238 grams of Miralax mixed with a 64-ounce bottle of lime or lemon Gatorade. Absolutely not raspberry Gatorade, because the red color might leave a blood-like residue.

I bought the Miralax well in advance at Walgreens and put the container on the counter in back of the goods of a man in line in front of me. He turned in my direction and said in Yiddish *"Abi gezundt"* (Be healthy).

"How did you know I'm Jewish?" I asked.

He pointed to the Miralax and said, "My girlfriend takes Miralax every day. She's Jewish."

The Miralax mix must be completely drunk by 11 p.m. the night before the procedure. Afterwards is a trip–or rather many trips. But by morning there isn't any soup left to eliminate, only a relatively light yellow liquid. Brown particles in the toilet bowl mean that the preparation has not been successful and that the doctor has to reschedule the colonoscopy.

My Delray Beach gastroenterologist is Dr. Theodore Doukides. He's quite superior in his knowledge, skill, and "bedside manner." I told him before the colonoscopy that my colon is very long. In the follow-up conversation, he said, "Ed, I appreciated the heads-up [no irony intended]. You sure didn't exaggerate."

To be sure, he couldn't get the scope through the loops; and I, therefore, had to have a "virtual colonoscopy" a few hours after the regular one for images of the areas deep within where, truly, "the sun doesn't shine." No illumination from the Sunshine duo sheds light there. The "virtual" was shorter than an MRI; I think it fell into the "cat-scan" category. But shorter though it was, it was not a picnic. (Note that a "not-picnic" has two "k" sounds.) Two strong technicians administered it; they had to turn me over and back twice, and I needed every bit of their strength.

First, one of the two inserted a balloon into my rectum and inflated it for the purpose of expanding the colon and making the surfaces more visible for the imaging. Of course, I was grateful for the technology. A somewhat similar procedure, I think, could be used for the doctor to remove interior polyps, if necessary. Whatever the discomfort of the air, the balloon method is easier than surgery. I will long remember the technicians' repeated instructions, "Hold your butt-cheeks together," to keep the balloon inside–a minor inconvenience, considering the alternative.

It took a full 48 hours afterwards, however, for all the air to come out. And come out it did–in periodic very loud blasts. I was worried that the noises–in the middle of the night–would awaken Reva and, also, neighbors. I actually had a fleeting concern that a sheriff would bang on the door and give me a citation for being a "public disturbance."

In sum, though, my complete colonoscopy experience–as are those of others–was very beneficial, even though it involved drama.

My New Grave

I recall that ever since I was very young my parents used to pride themselves on having pre-arranged their own funerals. Apparently, their own parents hadn't done so and the deaths caused financial stress for them and their siblings. They wanted to spare my brother and me that burden. My father died in 1987 and my mother, in 2000. With money inherited from my mother, I paid debts and took care of my "pre-need." It wasn't difficult. I went to Goldsteins' Rosenberg's Raphael-Sacks Inc. on North Broad St. in Philadelphia and had the good fortune to meet none other than the patriarch of the Goldstein family, Mr. Bennett Goldstein. He steered me through the financial arrangements. I got on an installment plan, which I paid in full over five years.

A lot of water has flowed under the bridge since 2005. I have moved to Delray Beach, Florida. I met a wonderful woman here and got married to her–my wife Reva. Lo and behold, she has arranged her funeral at the Beth Israel Cemetery in Woodbridge, New Jersey. Of course, we each hope and pray that we will live for many more years; but "pre-need" is "pre-need," and that is an essential expense, which should be dealt with, sooner rather than later. Reva's arrangement has been finalized. Mine, it turns out, has needed revision.

I told Reva that I want to be buried next to her–in New Jersey. Her first reaction was gratitude, but her second was conditional, "You're gonna have to keep your cubic feet clean! I mean to have the same high standards for our eternal resting area as I do for our home on earth."

More stipulations followed, such as "You can't bring your laptop inside with you."

And a requirement: "You'll have to wear your hearing aid and have a supply of new batteries."

And, finally, a recommendation: "It would be a good idea to bring Dramamine for the long trip from Florida to Philadelphia and the last leg to Woodbridge."

The Memorial Counselor in Woodbridge, Mr. Rocco Melchionna, was very personable. He worked hard to find two adjacent plots, necessitating his changing Reva's location. In the course of the telephone exchanges, I mentioned the three most important needs of Reva to him. Though they weren't so funny to me, I didn't mind if he got a chuckle from them. He, in turn, praising me for taking care of arrangements in advance, told me a humorous story about a widow whose husband hadn't done so.

Her husband died suddenly, and she had to cash in an annuity to pay for the funeral. The principal was $50,000. The basic funeral expenses amounted to $10,000. A week later, in discussing matters with her best friend, she announced that she was completely broke. The friend reacted, "You told me that the basic funeral cost was $10,000! What happened to the $40,000 remaining in the annuity?!"

"I had to buy a memorial stone."

"How could a memorial stone possibly cost $40,000?"

"It was seven carats!"

Three Quips

I continue my "Humor" section with these three short items. They might be considered as belonging to the "Word Play" section; but since the first two are vulgar, I haven't wanted to compromise that section's purity. Also, I need to allow fastidious readers to close the book at the outset and not have anything more to do with me. I anticipate quips sections in future books. I'm thinking of calling them "Quippes."

Leaving class one day, a student paused at the door and asked me, "We don't know what to call you. Is it 'Mr. Levenson' or 'Dr. Levenson'"? I replied, "It doesn't matter to me in the slightest. Just don't call me 'Asshole'!"
(I have been criticized that the curse word demeaned me as a teacher. I feel that, on the contrary, it enhanced my rapport with the students.)

Another time a student approached me standing at the door five minutes before the end of class and moved directly towards me indicating with a hand motion that I should step aside and let him leave the room. "Out of my way, pussy!" he ordered.
I countered, "Why are you insulting your mother?"
He, in turn, stated, "I'm not insulting my mother. I'm insulting *you*". But after hesitating, he asked, "What did you mean by that?"
He had given me a "teaching moment." An incredible mini-lesson followed about metaphor, at the conclusion of which a handshake ensued.

I had a routine in class in which I asked the rhetorical question "What do you think I am? Stupid!" and then after a brief pause said, "Don't answer that!"

Recently, I reenacted the seven-word question to my wife Reva and–before giving me the chance to say the "Don't answer that!"–she answered, "Yes!"

WORD PLAY

A Spelling Challenge

In March 2016 I wanted to help my wife Reva make a roundtrip flight reservation from West Palm Bcach to Charlotte, North Carolina, and back. I contacted Expedia; and, since Reva had never used the service, she let me do the talking with the Customer Service Representative (CSR). The basic arrangement proved relatively simple: direct flights to and from, times, and choice of seats. The spelling of Reva's name was another story, because the CSR had a different accent from mine.

CSR: "We need to have the exact spelling of your wife's full name, since it is not yet in our system."

Eddie: "OK."

CSR: "What is her name? Say it slowly, syllable by syllable."

Eddie: "OK. Re/Va Lu/Xen/Berg. She's an author, and that's her authorial name–without her married name 'Levenson' added to it."

CSR: "Thank you. Would you please spell her first name first?"

Eddie: "OK. R-E-V-A."

CSR: "Is the first letter 'L' as in 'Lion'...?"

Eddie: "No. 'R' as in 'rooster.' Then, 'E' as in 'elephant," 'V' as in 'veterinarian,' and 'A' as in 'ant.'"

CSR: "Let me repeat that: 'R' as in 'rooster,' 'E' as in 'elephant,' 'B' as in 'bedroom,' and 'A' as in 'ant.'"

Eddie: "No. You got the third one wrong. Not 'B' as in 'bedroom,' but 'V' as in 'Victor.'"

CSR: "Oh, I thought you said something different. So, it's 'R' as in 'rooster,' 'E' as in 'elephant,' 'V' as in 'Victor,' and 'A' as in 'ant.'"

Eddie: "Yes, now you've got it!"

CSR: "OK. Now I'm ready for your wife's last name. Is the first letter 'R' as in 'rooster'?"

Eddie: "No. It's 'L' as in 'lion.'"

CSR: "I'm sorry. Is the second letter 'A' as in 'arm'?"

Eddie: "No, it's 'U' as in 'umbrella.'"

CSR: "And are the next two letters 'C' and 'S'?"

Eddie: "We need to take one letter at a time. The next letter is an 'X' as in 'xylophone.'"

CSR: "Don't you mean a 'Z'?"

Eddie: "I *did* mean an 'X.' I should have said 'X' as in 'x-ray.'"

CSR: "I see, and next comes an 'E' as in 'elephant.'"

Eddie: "Yes, like the one in my wife's first name.

CSR: "Next, an 'M' as in 'man.'"

Eddie: "No. Many people make that mistake; I used to myself. It's an 'N' as in 'nut,' like someone who needs to have his head examined."

CSR: "Thank you, Mr. Levenson. And next a 'V' as in 'Victor.'"

Eddie: "No, a 'B' as in 'bedroom.'"

CSR: "And is the next an 'E' as in 'elephant,' as we have seen twice before?"

Eddie: "We're getting there. Yes, it's a third 'E.' I must note that, despite the three 'E's as in 'elephant,' my wife is really rather slim, even though she keeps worrying that she's not. An 'R' for 'rooster' follows. Finally, a 'G' for the two 'G's in 'God is good!'"

CSR: "I just want to repeat the whole thing to make sure I've gotten the spelling of both names right."

Eddie: "OK. You've been very conscientious and helpful, and I have as much patience as you do. But after we wrap this transaction up, would you please refer me to your supervisor. I would like to recommend you for a promotion."

CSR: [after repeating–correctly, to my great relief–the thirteen letters of "R-E-V-A L-U-X-E-N-B-E-R-G" with respective "as in's"]: "Mr. Levenson, thank you very much. I am now connecting you with my supervisor"

Supervisor: "How can I help you, Mr. Levenson?"

Ed: "Well, I am impressed with the conscientiousness and thoroughness of your Customer Service Representative, and I want to recommend her for a promotion."

Supervisor: "Thank you very much, Mr. Levenson. I am noting that you are satisfied with Expedia today. But I am afraid that the Customer Service Representative is not eligible for a promotion. She is still in training."

AUM

A friend of mine sometimes criticizes me for bestowing excessive praise on a person for something; but, be that as it may, I am not deterred from saying that the folks at AUM Computers in Delray Beach, Florida, are the best computer repair technicians it has ever been my privilege to deal with. Not wishing to get into a long discussion on the subject, I will simply say, "Bring your computer to them and you will see."

Apart from my high esteem for AUM Computers and its people, I have marveled at the beauty I appreciate in word plays on AUM-associated names. "AUM" itself, which is a very sacred sound in Hinduism signifying penetrating to the mysteries of the transcendent realm has a remarkable correspondence with the Hebrew root "*AYM*," which means "be in awe of."

The head of the company is Murji. He is, in fact, Hindu. When I first met him, I quipped that his name sounded a little like "Moshie," a Jewish nickname for "*Mosheh*" (Moses). He replied, "I answer to that also."

Murji's wife is Anjni. That name reminds me of "angel," and she certainly strikes me as one. For that matter, as two or three in one. It also resembles the name of the Hindu god of fire, Agni, protector of humanity; and fire evokes for me the Burning Bush of Exodus chapter 3 "which is not consumed."

A partner is Eli. The word corresponds in Hebrew either to the word spelled with an "*aleph*" meaning "my God" or a different word spelled with an "*ayin*" meaning "high one."

"Kishor" is a no-brainer. Heaven forbid that you think I consider him challenged in intelligence. On the contrary to the tenth power. I mean that the name sounds like a cognate of "kosher."

Finally, I want to mention Tim, short for "Timothy." The name comes from the Greek "*timotheos*," meaning "God-fearing." That was a derivative of the Hebrew "*y're Hashem*." Tim no longer works for AUM, but I remember him warmly.

AUM thus represents for me multicultural and multilingual serendipity over and above professional computer-repair know-how. [Email from Murji to Eddie on December 28, 2020. Thank you for being a person who sees connections that go past cultures and religions." Murji had mentioned that Anjni was "named after the mother of Hanuman, the god of wind." "Wind," in Hebrew is "*ru'aḥ*," which also means "spirit." This epithet evokes for me Moses' rare appellation for God in Numbers 16:22 and 27:16 "*Elohei haruḥot l'khol basar*" (God of the spirits of all flesh).]

El Español y Yo

I leave the title untranslated because I wish to avoid the ungrammatical "Spanish and Me." "*El español y yo*" in Spanish means "Spanish and I." My use of Spanish in my Latino teaching environment in Philadelphia from 2007 to 2012 was an adventure. A colleague of mine once remarked–or, perhaps, advised–that whereas she would never speak in a second language unless she were 100 per cent sure of the correctness of her usages, the complete opposite is true of me. What follows, among other things, are "whoppers" of mistakes I have made. In most cases, they are simply "jokes on me"; but once an ill-chosen word offended a colleague. I conclude the first part of this essay with an anecdote about a rather interesting Spanish mistake made by a non-Latino student–not a mistake of mine.

All of the coming names are pseudonyms; but, in calling the first student Yousef Ismail, I preserve the flavor of his Palestinian real name. He was sitting in the far left back corner of the room when into class five minutes late walked Francisco Colon. Yousef waved to him across the room, greeting him with, "*Francisco, qué pasó?*"

Francisco smiled and waved back, whereupon I attempted a friendly correction: "Yousef, '*qué pasó?*' [what happened?] is OK; but '*qué pasa?*' [what's happening?] would be better."

He replied, "I know, I know, but there's no big difference."

"But there *is* a difference," I countered. He repeated, "I know"; and he added a very interesting explanation: "'*Pasó*' is masculine, '*pasa*' is feminine, so '*pasó*' goes with Francisco."

The offense I caused was when I greeted a female teacher as "*mi amiguita.*" I really thought that in using a diminutive of "*amiga,*" I was saying "friendly female acquaintance." I understand that she could have taken the word that way. She, however, retorted that she was not my "girlfriend." In this vein, I once made a terrible mistake in referring to a student as "*mamacita.*" Rosa used to strike me as being very strong when boys started to mess with her. All she had to do was stare them down while raising her left forefinger. I asked her once whether she had brothers.

"Yes," she replied. "Four, to be exact." "Well, that partly explains your strength," I replied; and then, thinking I was expressing something like "Rosa is our young class mother," I said, "*Rosa está nuestra mamacita.*" Rosa gave me an uncomfortable look, which I did not understand. A student many weeks later explained to me that "*mamacita*" connotes "hot ticket."

To be sure, not all of my forays into Spanish were out-and-out mistakes. Once I actually coined a Spanish word that I had never heard before. Juan was a young 13-year-old student newly arrived from Ecuador. Every morning he refused to push his hood back. I tried a different approach for days in succession in my attempts to enforce his compliance with the District's no-hat policy. First, I stated the rule to Juan. I pointed to the hood the day after. The day after that I simply said, "The hood!" He shooed me off with his right hand. On the fourth day I said, "Juan, if the principal walks in and sees what you're wearing, I'm in trouble"; and he replied, "That's your problem!" I thought that I might subsequently have better luck in Spanish; and so, finding the word for "hood" in the dictionary, I next tried, "*La capucha*!"–but to no avail.

Now comes my *tour de force*. It was the sixth day. I looked at Juan, hooded as ever; and, from deep in my unconscious, I uttered, "*Capuchito*!!" Juan was stunned. With eyes blazing, he raised his voice, "Don't call me that!"

I hadn't expected any reaction from him at all, but I realized on the spot that he might have given me a new opportunity; and so he had. I said, "Of course, Juan, I won't call you that again, but you have to take your hood off." And he did, shaking his fist at me, "Don't ever call me that ever again!" To everyone's surprise, when his hood was off, out flowed a beautiful head of long black hair over a newly visible handsome face. The girl to his right was so taken that she jumped up, put her arms around his head, and exclaimed, "*Mira, está guapo*!" (Look, he's handsome!)

Juan, embarrassed, squirmed from under her arms and sunk lower in his seat.

The next day he was not in class; and, then, he was absent for two whole weeks. I grew concerned, worrying that I might have precipitated some kind of emotional breakdown. But, in truth, he had simply gone on a trip to Ecuador. Lo and behold, first thing in the morning of the Monday of the third week, three students came rushing into my room exclaiming, "Dr. Levenson, *capuchito* is back!"

At the beginning of our class a period later, Juan took his seat and upbraided me sharply, "I told you not to call me that"; and I had to protest to him that I hadn't, for it was all his friends' doing.

To this day, I am perplexed why the word upset him so much. A Spanish-speaking colleague actually suggested that he might have interpreted the word not as "little boy with the hood," but as "little boy from where they wear hoods," "hoodies" being a socioeconomic mark of identification.

Another colleague, on the other hand, offered the analysis that Juan might have thought I said "*capullito*," (with two "*ll*"s), attempting to pronounce the two "*ll*"s as "zh," "*capuzhito.*" "*Capullo*" means "bud," and "*capullito*" would mean "little bud." But on another level the word can have, according to my 275,000-word Oxford Spanish dictionary, a very vulgar colloquial metaphorical meaning. Juan might have thought I meant, "Little dickhead!" A friend in Florida clarified further that that the meaning is much worse than that, for, whereas "dickhead" means "jerk" in English, "*capullito*" among Latinos is a vicious gay slur.

I don't have to stress here that there is a very important lesson in my colleague's suggestion about the need for caution on the part of a person trying to express herself or himself in a second language.

"Less" is Indeed Less

Have you ever heard the paradoxes "More is less and less is more"? Critics have often quoted the second one to me when I talk too much. That condition may be called "logorrhea" in a loose (no double meaning originally intended) unclinical usage of the term. That play on words may be the only real justification for my including this piece in my "Word Play" [of my recent *Genres Mélange Deuxième* section]. On the other hand, my title indicates a paradox.

And, thirdly, I am analyzing a mistake made by two Major League Baseball sportscasters in broadcasting baseball "plays," namely, homeruns.

I cannot reveal the city, the league, the team, and the perpetrators—both to spare the guilty and to protect myself from the legal charges of defamation and hearsay, though, yes, I am willing to swear under oath that I heard the perps say it not once, but several times. And, in fact, I have letters from each of the two perps thanking me for sending them the correction for what they had been saying.

The mistake is the modifier "less" in connection with the countable noun "homeruns," as in, "The shortstop has hit less homeruns this year than last year." "Less," analogous to "much," modifies uncountable items. With countable items the correct modifier is "fewer," analogous to "many." Publix supermarkets, to their enduring credit, get the word right in the respective sign over the checkout aisle for "fewer than ten items."

During a rain delay I wrote letters to the sportscasters informing them of the mistake. I received a very courteous thank you from each and a promise to use the correct word henceforth. Did they do so? Not a whit. They were old dogs who couldn't learn a new trick. At least insofar as I monitored them. Perhaps they used the correct word "fewer" when I wasn't watching the games.

[Update on 09/02/2018. My brother Rob has informed me that one of the two sportscasters mentioned has begun to use the correct word.]

Pool Conversation

I bet you thought from the title that the conversation was around the swimming pool.

Incorrect! It was on the sidelines of a pool table in the Clubhouse Pool Room. My son Judah was here on vacation. Rest assured that Reva and I registered him as a guest. He loved taking long walks all around Kings Point, having lunch in East End Cafe, swimming in the other kind of pool, and, especially, playing pool with our neighbor John and the other regulars every other morning.

One person we met was Seymour Franklin, who we learned is a Kings Point veteran of 45-years duration. I was interested in observing the games. Four players paired off in teams of two each, and Seymour and I began a conversation, punctuated only by his taking his shots every fourth turn. I cautioned him that one of my biggest faults is that I talk too much and that he should feel free to beg off when he would get tired of me, but he said, "No problem; I enjoy talking with you."

Early on, I blurted out a question, "Do you know what a privy well is?"

"Why on earth are you asking me that? As a matter of fact I do!"

I explained that my next article in *Kings Point News* [published in *EHAM*] was to be about the privy well I discovered in my Philadelphia backyard and that I had a catchy introduction for the piece: "Whereas the privy well of Ben Franklin [your namesake] is historical, mine is history, for it no longer exists."

Seymour told me that he had discovered a privy well on his property in Elmont, New York, and that he used to dispose of junk in it. I hope that the municipality won't come chasing after him now with a citation that he had been violating an ordinance.

"Do you know where the name 'Franklin' came from?" he asked. "Believe me, I'm no relation of Ben Franklin. When my mother came through Ellis Island in 1898, she didn't know a word of English. The immigration officer asked her what her name was and she didn't understand his question and couldn't answer. An assistant extracted a long name beginning with 'F.' On the basis of that, the officer told her that her name in America would be 'Franklin.'"

"Do you have a nickname?"

"Yeah, 'Si!' You want to hear a story about that nickname?"

"Sure!"

"I was a jewelry manufacturer on Canal Street. My partner and I had 18 workers, and we too went out on sales. My territory included Northern Long Island, but I traveled as far west as Chicago. Once I visited a proprietor in Great Neck named Seymour Trager. I entered his store, approached his counter, and greeted him, 'Good morning, Seymour!'

"To my utter astonishment, he exploded. 'Don't you ever call me "Seymour" again! I'm "Si! Si! Si! Si!"'" [Editor's note: Correct punctuation for a quote within a quote within a quote is double quotation marks within single quotation marks within double quotation marks.]

"'Well I'm 'Seymour! . . . Seymour! Seymour! Seymour!' I went home, threw out all my Seymour 'Si' Franklin business cards, and had new ones printed with only the names 'Seymour Franklin.' That's an interesting episode in the saga of Seymour Franklin."

"Seymour, there's an irony here for me. I feel an instant warm friendship with you, but I have to say I understand Si Trager, although I don't condone his loss of temper. My authorial name for *Kings Point News* has been 'Ed,' but I much prefer my nickname 'Eddie.'

"My name 'Edward' has been a problem for me all my life because I have felt that it sounds harsh. In my family I grew up with 'Edward-and-Nothing-But-Edward.' A friend of mine called up once and asked, 'Is Eddie there?'

"My mother, God bless her, answered, 'There's no one with that name here;' and she hung up."

Scrabble Slaughter

Early 2016.

Reva Luxenberg and I, newlyweds, are Scrabble aficionados. We play two games of Scrabble every day. Though I was a capable player in my youth, I have encountered in Reva a formidable opponent; and, truth to tell, I am embarrassed to say that she beats me three games out of four. According to the statistics kept by the computerized Scrabble Complete program, I have won in the last three months only 46 victories to her 184!

I haven't been losing without strenuous protests. Above all, I have a visceral revulsion against *The Official Scrabble Dictionary* (*OSD*), which I believe Reva has memorized *in toto* and often reviews secretly. To my thinking, this cockamamie concoction includes words in different languages from all corners of the globe which aren't English and shouldn't be considered loan words in English, like "*khat*" (an Arabian shrub); "*poilu*" (a World War I French infantry soldier); or "*xu*" (a monetary unit of Vietnam). The *OSD* even lists the *names* of letters in several languages such as English, Hebrew, and Greek: "ef," "ar," and "es"; "*gimel*," "*zayin*," and "*pe*"; and "*eta*," "*ksi*," and "*mu*," respectively.

A few weeks ago my brother Rob called on the phone from Philadelphia just as Reva and I were sitting down to play. "Rob," I said, "I can't talk long now because Reva and I are settling into our nightly Scrabble ritual slaughter."

When he asked what I meant, I told him about Reva's prowess in the game, and I related the Won-Loss, or rather the Loss-Won, ratio at that time.

"I'm astonished, Ed," he replied. "You were an excellent Scrabble player when Ma, Dad, you, and I used to play during our teens. You remember how good Dad was, and yet you used to win as often as he did."

"How can I ever forget Dad's proficiency?" I said. "Remember the time he scored 165 points on one word, putting the letters

'Q-U-A-V-E-R-S' down horizontally on the bottom-middle Triple Word Score, with the 'Q' on a Double Letter Score and the 'S' linking to a vertical 'C-L-I-F-F-S,' and using all seven letters for a 50-point 'Bingo.' We needed to send that total for the consideration of *The Guinness Book of World Records.* As for me, since I am downtrodden in Scrabble now, perhaps I have repressed memories of any earlier Scrabble glory of mine."

"But then," I continued, "Reva is truly brilliant. I can't take that away from her. And she has a very rich background. Not only has she attended writers' conferences in different places in America and England, but she has traveled extensively and picked up new words wherever she has gone. The trouble is that she has internalized them as being mainstream English!"

I would not do myself justice if I did not mention The Look. If I put on the board a decent move yielding 15 or more points and Reva feels I could have gotten at least 10 more points elsewhere with the same letters, she looks at me sideways in disapproval. I remember from my teaching days in inner-city Philadelphia that "looking at someone sideways" was an action presaging an impending assault. Reva's intention with 'The Look is never violent; but I interpret it as a mixture of helpfulness, condescension, and [double ellipse]... ... pity. The last is the hardest to bear. Similarly, Reva often muses that she feels terrible about my bruised ego and that she feels impelled to "throw" some games. That would be even more unacceptable.

Eight months later.

Among the adjustments newlyweds make in the first year of marriage, Reva and I have made beneficial ones in our Scrabble playing. First of all, we now use the *Merriam-Webster's Collegiate Dictionary* as our word arbiter, not The *Official Scrabble Dictionary.* Secondly, Reva has conditioned herself not to give me The Look. Thirdly, I am making peace with my losing ratio, recognizing that my satisfactions in playing Scrabble are very different from Reva's. Namely, it is far more important for me to form longer words to open up the board in spread-out patterns than to be compulsive about point totals. Though I continue to loathe such words as "za" (meaning "pizza"), I have become comfortable with the Chinese "*qi*" (life force).

Above all, I have a sense of fulfillment that I have been learning much English. I am not too thrilled about archaisms like "et" (ate) and "ane" (one); but they do, just the same, add to my store of knowledge. And, last but not least, our Scrabble ritual–followed frequently by watching a DVD–is enhancing our sharing, companionship, and love wonderfully.

To "Burke"

I have been attending the Kings Point "Open Mike" events of the Sociables Club in the Clubhouse on Thursday nights to read stories and/or do karaoke; and Reva accompanies me when she can. It's great fun; and I have come to recognize that I genuinely enjoy the two-hour entertainment. There's real talent in the community, and I have found myself sitting back and forgetting my cares.

Recently resident Michelle Burke sang three very beautiful songs. By chance when the "show" was over and we all were going our separate ways, I passed Michelle in the parking lot outside of East End Cafe. She was standing alone waiting for her ride, and I stopped to compliment her on her singing.

But, as I often do, I made "small talk."

"Michelle, do you know that your last name is an English verb—'to burke.'"

"I had no idea," she replied, "What does it mean?"

"It means, 'to suppress something, not to let something make waves,' as in 'to burke an inquiry' or 'to burke an issue.'"

"How interesting!"

"It is, indeed. But I'm not so happy how the word came to mean what it does. For the verb is based on the political views of the 18th-century British M.P. (Member of Parliament) and writer Edmund Burke, a conservative (with a small "c"), who praised the British system of government for its embodiment of gradual evolutionary change, as opposed to the radical revolutionary upheaval of the French system.

"The poet Samuel Taylor Coleridge, who was critical of Burke for a number of things, among which was his conservatism, wrote a poem 'To Burke'; and I believe the title of the poem came to be interpreted as a verb. What bothers me is that the verb has the negative connotation of 'shoving something important under the rug,' whereas Edmund

Burke's disenchantment with the horrors resulting from the French Revolution was sensible."

"Well, then, from now on," she replied, "I'll certainly 'burke' 'burkers,' but I'll be careful not to do so in my own name." (This piece has been slightly fictionalized.)

Two Southern European Phrases

I have had happy experiences–ten years apart–with phrases in a South-Slavic language and an Indo-European one. They are Serbo-Croatian and Albanian, respectively. My readers know how much I enjoy the richness of ethnicity. I like to ask people to whom I am introduced–particularly restaurant servers–whether they will tell me, or whether I may guess, their ethnic identities.

Well, I was recently in the hospital to receive intravenous antibiotic for a foot infection. (I learned quite a bit there about my Diabetes Type Two, but that is another story.)

One of the doctors who treated me was an infectious-diseases specialist. When she introduced herself to me, I got permission from her and asked if she was Latina. Missing on that one and sensing that she may have been Eastern European, I took the safe guess of Russian.

"No," she said, "I'm from Croatia."

Having a veritable "Eureka" memory, I raised my right hand and exclaimed "*Moia ruka*!" (my hand).

Astounded, she paused five seconds and then asked how I had come to know that phrase.

"Doctor," I confessed, "don't think I'm such a polymath. Those are the only two words in Serbo-Croatian that I know. I learned them 58 years ago, I think of them occasionally, and I will never forget them."

"Who taught them to you and where was it?"

"Well, doctor, I am more moved than I can say to relate the story. It was in a Jewish Education class at the Boston Hebrew Teachers College (HTC) in Brookline, Massachusetts. It was in the fall of 1960. The teacher was a prominent Hebrew-language expert, and he was introducing to the class the innovative approach of teaching 'Hebrew Through Pictures.' The pictures were stick-figures projected on a screen.

"One day, the teacher–who had been educated at Harvard's Department of Education–brought a Harvard friend who was an expert in the teaching of Serbo-Croatian. The friend taught us for one hour 'Serbo-Croatian Through Pictures.' The purpose was for the class to experience the fun of learning a completely new language via the innovative method and thereby to identify with it better. I learned '*moia ruka*' in that class and never forgot the words, as you see."

"Well, since I'm examining your foot, I'll teach you a third Serbo-Croatian word, the one for 'foot'; and I'm sure you'll never forget that one either. It's '*noga*.' '*Moia noga*' means 'my foot.'"

I got excited. "Doctor, there's an incredible bi-lingual play on words here! In Hebrew '*nogah*' means 'light!' Its range of meaning extends to 'spiritual light' and 'heavenly light.' It is also the Hebrew name for Venus, which is the brightest planet. I am making metaphorical connections in my mind between your benevolent presence and the radiance of Heaven–and your help in the blessed curing of my foot.

About ten years ago in Philadelphia I taught in the afternoon "Twilight-School Program" after regular school was over. The hours were three to six p.m. My classes were on the first floor, and I generally went up to my fourth-floor classroom at the end of the day to gather up my belongings before leaving for home. I often encountered on the fourth floor night-shift custodial workers, subcontracted by the School District, cleaning–even in my room itself, and often a team of the same two women. As it happened, the custodial workers, at least the ones I met, were all Albanian. The women taught me "good night" in Albanian–"*Naten amir.*"

One morning I parked in the back parking lot of the school and entered the building through the adjacent basement. An Albanian (male) custodian on the day shift happened to be sweeping the entrance way. As he paused to let me pass, I waved and greeted him with a cheerful "*Naten amir.*" Very surprised, he looked at me in some confusion and couldn't find the words for a reply.

Recognizing that I had said "good night" to him when it was morning, I explained, "Look, those are the only two words in Albanian that I know!"

"Oh," he recovered his composure, "I thought you were talking to me in English!"

Thinking back on that exchange, I recognize that it contains a powerful lesson about the components of understanding language. Context and expectations are all-important. The custodian never dreamed that I would say anything in Albanian to him, let alone "good night" in the morning. Furthermore, he didn't have enough confidence in his English to be certain that the four syllables of "*Naten amir*" were not English words.

A more important lesson than word comprehension, dear readers, is also involved. The custodian and I appreciated our shared humanity. My speaking to him in Albanian, however absurd my intentional mistake was, bridged a cultural divide.

POETRY

A Poem for Grieving Friends and Loved Ones

by son Judah Levenson

When is where you walk with a lilt down Market to
brunch after a morning at the piano
Where you sat the nails exposed through wooden stairs
but a field of flowers continually suggested
When a stray mark an accident rips through your gaze
the image of makeup ugly and pretty
Where a life devoted to new music and nurturing pills
muddy indoors playing bodies early evening
When you were in town briefly so bad might know only
laughter or a fight for friendship
Where the image of yourself as protector dissolves
because nothing stop the synth shared plates
When is where you saw the child and afraid of
abandonment held him seeing you the only photo
Where you're tucked in bed in the back shack with
warmth satisfaction candles gardening books
When remnants of hurt all around you read Anne
Carson's myth and consider being a stranger
Where is stronger Kassandra yourself screaming not
wanted looked into the camera recently
When you were embarrassed by what to trust but this
string of affections could be a beginning
Where disaster is a consideration who should fear the
way you move a block blocked value
When being memory being easy to hide in empty in
other people's buildings are we too comfortable

[In my discussion below my references to lines are based on an earlier
layout in which the couplets that you see took up long horizontal

single lines. Thus the line references here must be understood as referring to couplets.]

I am deeply honored to try my hand at analyzing Judah's *avant garde* poetry. My first attempt at the genre was with his "Anscha" in my *"Edward's Humor" and More* and my second was with the alliteration of this poem in my *Genres Mélange Deuxième*. I begin this treatment afresh, hoping to achieve a holistic understanding of the poem in one sitting. I recognize that I may well need to revisit it further in the future.

The first thing that strikes me is the structure of thirteen lines introduced, alternatingly, by the relative/interrogative words "when" or "where." As lines 1 and 7 specifically indicate, the temporal and the spatial ideas overlap, and that appears to me to be the case in several other lines as well, such as in the "where" of line 4 which ends with "early evening" or the "when" of line 1 which is localized on Market Street (I presume this is Center City Philadelphia's east-west axis).

The choice of 13 lines appears to me to be a conscious choice on Judah's part to differentiate the poem's length from that of a sonnet; and his purpose for that, accordingly, may be to weight the poem with seven "when's and six "where's–"bookending" it with the "when's and thus subtly indicating that that dimension is the more important one of the two.

So when did important memories take place? As in the case of "Anscha" when (and where) I myself had memories of visiting Judah's dying grandmother in the nursing home. I remember Judah being "afraid of abandonment" (line 7) in the face of the immanent divorce of his parents with "remnants of hurt all around" (line 9). "Stronger Kassandra yourself" (line 10) strikes me as an uncanny past association of mine with my own identification with the slave woman of King Agamemnon facing death at the hands of the murderous Queen Clytaemnestra in Aeschylus' *Oresteia*. I wonder if Judah might not be an alter ego of mine in touch with innermost mysteries of *my* history.

And yet the poem reflects joys of a present life as well: "a morning at the piano" (line 1); "a field of flowers" (line 2); "new music" and "playing bodies" (line 4); "laughter" (line 5); "image of yourself as protector" (line 6); "tucked in bed in the back shack with warmth satisfaction candles gardening books" (line 8); and "this string of affections could be a beginning" (line 11).

But conflict and ambivalence are in the poet's consciousness as well: "an accident rips through your gaze the image of makeup ugly and pretty" (line 3); "nurturing pills muddy indoors" (line 4); and "a fight for friendship" (line 5).

To be sure, though the poet ends the poem with the rhetorical "are we too comfortable," I think he rather betrays feelings of discomfort and loneliness, as well as fear of invisibility, in the participial clause "being easy to hide in empty other people's buildings."

As I wrote, the poem bears revisiting, perhaps in connection with others that Judah might earmark for consideration together with this one.

Postscript on December 27, 2018. Judah has encouraged my interaction with the poem even to the point of my interjecting my own clear personal associations into it. How about my making a play on the "synth shared plates" of line 6 with the "Synch" of my title *Genres Synch*. Not only are Judah and I "in sync" but we are doing a "synthesis." Secondly, dear readers, consider the uncanny inter-amplifications between my study of the "Mythos and Truth" of Euripides' *Herakles* in my "Interpretation" section of *Genres Synch* and "When remnants of hurt all around you read Anne Carson's myth and consider being a stranger" (line 9).

"A Sonnet in a Pinch"–As a Teaching Tool in Our Writing Club

Explanation of my book title *Genres Synch,* mentioned in line 4: "Synch" (from "synchronize") is the original form of "sync." The "ch," from the Greek letter "*chi*" is thus, originally, hard. It is a play on the French "*cinq*" or the Spanish "*cinco*," which means "five." The title alludes to the fact that the book is my fifth. The word is also a play on "cinch" in both the meanings of "easy"/"serendipitous" and "belt fastener"/ "connecting." I, accordingly, intend the soft "ch" pronunciation here.

Rhyme scheme: abba cddc effe gg
Meter: iambic pentameter (da DA, da DA, da DA, da DA, da DA)
Hendecasyllabic lines (that is, having an eleventh syllable): 2, 3, 5, 6, 7, 8, 9, 11, 12,
The "near rhymes" of the c and f lines are not inartistic, as in the poems of Emily Dickinson.

1 I've had to write this sonnet in a pinch   a   in my substitution of six writings here
2 A poem crafted for your reading pleasure   b
3 My joys reflected for you without measure   b
4 In this the "Po(e)try" of my *Genres Synch.*   a   soft "ch" in "*Synch*"

5 My 'nspiring Muses are indeed two Williams   c
6 Shakespeare and father Levenson in Heaven   d   "William Julius Levenson" in full
7 Revering both I'm now a deeper *maven*"   d   Yiddish for "someone in the know"
8 Of hard-won truths of life which bring fulfillment.   c

9 The love of Reva Spiro [a metaphorical teenager here] and of Judah   e   "Spiro" was Reva's birth name

44

10 Sustains my spirit time and time again   f
11 Of Rob, Loudell, Aliza, and young Benj(a)min   f   brother, sister-
in-law, daughter, son
12 And many, many more I cannot tell ya.

13 I pinch myself, "Did I just write this stuff?   g
14 A poet I've become pr'haps good enough."   g

Forward at Sunset–December 16, 2018

In poems we often read of sunsets' sadness
Horizons' rosy glow with orange suns
Bright days departing and some rainy ones
Emotions of lives fading into darkness.

A walk today I had was full of joy
Ducklings fifteen at twilight o'er the lake
A royal palm diagonal like a stake[1]
I'm happy as a fifteen-year-old boy.

My manuscript of *Genres Synch*[2] submitted
In sync with Reva, children, readers too
For me no sorrow of the sunset was in view
To writing five more books I am committed.

For six to ten to God I pray for health
In life exulting, not at all for wealth.

---

[1] I'm referring to a palm on the shore of the lake at the footbridge on the southwest side of the Kings Point Clubhouse. It juts out at a 45-degree angle over the water.

[2] "Synch" is a play on the Latin/French/Spanish "*quinque*"/"*cinq*"/"*cinco*" (five). *Genres Synch* is my fifth Xlibris book.

L'Zekher Hamiqdash
(In Memory of the Sanctuary)

My title, dear readers, represents an important value of Judaism, commemoration of the two destructions of the Jerusalem Sanctuary, first by the Babylonians and later by the Romans.

There are two particularly important symbolizations of this value in Jewish religious life: the groom's breaking of the goblet underfoot at his wedding and leaving the façade of a new synagogue unfinished during construction. The customs have the deeper meaning that life's imperfections are challenges to be accepted and that human beings have the religious obligation to correct and improve–a marriage and community life, pointedly–starting with ourselves.

Readers may be interested in my article on Psalm 145 (*Genres Mélange,* pages 147-153), in which I theorized that the "*nun*"-verse was omitted "*l'zekher hamiqdash.*"

Ironically, I invoke this value in connection with the completion of this book [*Genres Synch*]. I want very much that it be published in calendar year 2018. A severe crisis, however, has beset me in this striving. I have structured the book according to a symmetry of eight items per section, as I have indicated in my "Preface"; but, at a very late moment, "Content Evaluation" [that is, on my end–not of Xlibris] has rejected six of the eight items I earmarked for this the "Poetry" section. So I began to improvise like crazy to find six substitute pieces.

Eureka!–I "eurekize" again. This essay will be my eighth item–a "Non-Number-Eight," the broken goblet, the blank part of the unfinished façade. Now all I need is to come up with five, not six, substitutions besides this one. And, miracle of miracles, I see my way doing it. More speedily than I had ever considered possible yesterday when in the throes of crisis.

Guess what, though. My verbosity calms my soul, and I want to share with you, for this purpose, something about transliterating Hebrew into English letters. The title of this piece affords me the opportunity to illustrate two technical points (with characteristic digressions, of course):

First, the *"kh"* in *"Zekher"* is the transliteration of the Hebrew letter *"khaf."* The *"q"* in *"Hamiqdash"* is the transliteration of the Hebrew letter *"qof"* as opposed to a *"k,"* which is the transliteration of a *"kaf."* A *"ḥet"* in Hebrew should not be confused with a *"khaf"* and must be transliterated by an *"ḥ"* with a subscript dot, as in my Hebrew name *"Yitsḥaq."*

Secondly, a word about digraphs in the transliteration. The letters in *"qd"* in *"Hamiqdash"* and *"tsḥ"* (this is not a trigraph, because the *"ts"* represents one letter, a *"tsadi"*) in *"Yitsḥaq"* are not digraphs, because the letters occur in different syllables.

One of my funniest experiences in my fulfilling relationship with Xlibris involves a proofreader's association of the letters "sh" with the transliteration of the Hebrew letter *"ḥet."* The mistake originated from a faulty direction I gave. The word in question was *"Ḥumash."* (the Five Books of Moses). The word came back in the galley proofs without the subscript dot under the first letter. I gave feedback in the respective note, "The *'h'* needs a subscript dot"; and I received back *"Humaṣh"* with the subscript dot under the final, not the initial, *"ḥ."* I related this experience in my piece "Hebrew Dots, and More," in *Genres Mélange,* page 38. Felicitously, I can now correct a terrible mistake I made in that place. I called the *"sh"* a "lexeme," whereas it is a "digraph."

And speaking of mistakes, I want to encourage readers to report any and all you discover to Xlibris. But while you are at that, you might also send reviews (hopefully favorable, or at least somewhat favorable) to Amazon.

To bookend this piece, my loving posterity might find the corrections valuable when publishing my collected works in commemorating the two-hundredth anniversary of my birth in 2142. I was born on February 17th, as was basketball great Michael Jordan, if anyone wants to send me a birthday present in 2019. And by all means send him one also, if you can locate him. On a couple of occasions I, without success, tried to contact him to tell him how proud I am to share his birthday.

My Family–Children

(iambic hexameter, mostly)

Josh, Judah, and Aliza, the youngest Benjamin–
Three sons, a daughter also–I'm the proudest father.
Thank God, they're healthy, kind, and truly want to win
By "being there" and helping all and one another.

Josh is very caring to Jen and Sophie and Caleb,
The best of all examples of a devoted family man.
Aliza, "favorite daughter," never has been a reb,
Had to put her out of order to fit the rhyme-scheme plan.

Now Judah, artist, teacher, literatus extraordinaire,
Makes drama come alive with humor, insight, and love,
Dyadic with his DAP–"Dad/*Abba/* and *Pater.*"
A line for Benjy here—Hear Hear!—and not above.

He's unsurpassed in service and diplomacies.
All four of these my children have wondrous qualities.

My Man: Anniversary and Valentine's Day Sonnet
by wife Reva

O yes! My man is one out of a billion,
Embodiment of a real dissident,
Emboldening in books at least a million,
Reflecting in his poems ingeniousment.

O yes! My man's a wondrous storyteller,
Gives many many smiles and bellylaughs,
Shares tales with males and females truly stellar,
With friends and guests and cafeteria staffs.

O yes! My man's names do indeed keep changing,
"EdWARD," "Eduardo," "Mister Ed," or "Eddie."[1]
But he's himself on solid ground maintaining,
Being always honest gen'rous true and steady.

So very powerful is my love, you see,
He's captured all my heart and all of me.

---

[1] He maintains that there was a stress on the last syllable of his parents' "Edward-and-only-Edward" persona for him, which demonstrated an unconscious controlling impulse on their part.

On *The Merchant of Venice*

The Merchant of Venice is a challenge for sure,
Why Shakespeare drew the hateful Shylock Jew
Conversion to Christian religion the only cure,
Spectators' fury aroused through and through.

An ethnographic panoply he does display
A Palatine[1], a Moor, an Englishman in Venice.
The latter is plain, he writes with mock dismay;
The bearded Jew gives ready usury service.

The "pound of flesh" as payment of a bond,
A penalty sought by someone quite demonic,
From whom his daughter needed to abscond,
Revenging and with Europe not harmonic.

This play of popularity exceeding,
Courageous moral judgment though is needing.

---

[1]   A royal courtier from a number of possible places in Europe.

Umbrella of Love
by Jeffrey Langer

No we have not met
I'm a friend of Edward
I mean Eddie
I don't mean to offend
He's somewhat touchy about that
Eddie's a gushing member
Of our writers group
Our secretary and supporter
Knowledgeable critiquer
Anthology editor
Passionate promoter
An obviously loving father
He asked me to write you a poem:
I'm all for a lesbian wedding
Men say I do and mean you do
Men pledge happily ever after
But mean until you grow old and fat
Men say equal but mean 80/20 their way
Men say what you want to hear
And have selective amnesia
I've always respected women
Because they say what they mean
And are loyal through and through
Every woman except one
So good luck walking hand in hand in life
As wife and wife
Smiling at the pain
Having each other
As an umbrella in the rain

FICTION

A Gunman in Publix

I was in a check-out line in the Oriole Plaza Publix after lunch one day in January. The store was moderately crowded, but the staff and the customers at that time of day were not unduly pressured. I was second in line and had my groceries and other goods ready on the conveyor belt behind a separator bar.

All of a sudden a man pushed into the line behind me, moved in front of me, put on a stocking mask, pulled out a gun from a left-side holster with his right hand, pointed it at the cashier (a young woman), and said to her–exactly as in cops-and-robbers movies– "This is a stick-up. Put all the paper money in this cloth bag. Nobody move, and nobody will get hurt."

I did some quick thinking, mainly that the robber intended a quick in-and-out job and that he really didn't want to hurt anyone. Also, that the stakes for him were not so high that if something went wrong, he wouldn't want to make a quick getaway without getting any loot.

I had considered coming up on him from the right and swiping my left arm upward (I am a lefty for actions requiring strength) to knock his right arm out of position–or faking cardiac arrest from the shock, pretend-fainting on the floor, and then toppling the candy rack on the right side of the check-out line onto him.

But I realized that either plan was dangerous because the robber might panic and shoot someone. The risk to people and the store's loss of money weren't worth it.

Then passivity on my part began to make sense for me. I had a confident thought that the robber wasn't very smart in that the odds of a successful haul for him were not great. There were at least 40 individuals all over the store at that time, many of whom he couldn't see; and the escape routes out both the front and back exits were long and circuitous. The police, summoned by alarms, would be closing in any second, especially inasmuch as the Sheriff's Headquarters is nearby off Cumberland Drive.

Sure enough, sirens soon began to wail on Atlantic Avenue and in Oriole Plaza; and, before anyone in the store could do anything, a policeman, previously unnoticed, shouted to the robber from behind the left wall in the Bakery Section, "Drop your gun now! We've got the place surrounded, and we shoot to kill! You don't have a chance!"

The robber groaned dejectedly and dropped his gun, whereupon three other policemen, who had been approaching from different directions, ordered him in turn to drop his bag and take off his mask, raise both arms high, and surrender. He was handcuffed and led out of the store to a patrol car.

The Store Manager approached to comfort the cashier, and she burst into tears in his arms.

Cleveland-Miami Round Trip

Unusual things happened in the Philadelphia School District. At the beginning of his service, Dave was shuffled around to different schools. One September he had to sit in the auditorium for three weeks until "leveling" of class size would be completed and he could be given a teaching roster. In August of 1997, he was "force transferred" to a new school; and, after waiting there in September with nothing to do, he was told "for his ears only" that the system was "severely distressed" and that he wouldn't be getting a roster in his area of appointment (Social Studies) until the first week of November. Since the uncertainty had been "making him sick," he reasoned, he called in sick for the period of the 1997 baseball World Series at the end of October.

The Series was between the Cleveland Indians and the Florida Marlins, teams he had been following. He decided to "go for broke," considering the situation "the chance of a lifetime"–pardon the clichés. He loved his 1994 GMC Jimmy–he still has it, by the way, and loves it all the more–bought a ticket online to the third game of the Series on Tuesday, October 21st, left Philadelphia at 4 a.m. very early that morning, and made it to Jacobs Field in Cleveland in time for the start of the game.

To his left were two Orthodox Jewish men wearing *yarmulkas* and *tsitsis* (fringes); and he heard them saying that they would love to celebrate the upcoming *Shmini Atseres* and *Simchas Torah* holidays with family in Coral Springs, Florida, on the Thursday and Friday of that week, and that then, if the Series would reach the seventh game–which would take place on the Sunday night of October 26th in Miami–"move heaven and earth" to get tickets to that.

Dave butted in, "Could you get a ticket for me also?"

"We can try, but how would you be getting there?"

One thing led to another, and another, and another–and the three of them piled into the Jimmy at the end of the game and embarked right then and there on the 17-hour trip to Coral Springs. There was no margin of error whatsoever, for the men had to arrive before the beginning of *yontiff* (the festival) at sundown of the next day. But it was very helpful that there were three of them to share the driving, allowing each to sleep when not behind the wheel.

The seventh game of the 1997 World Series did, in fact, take place; and it *was* "the game of a lifetime." It was a thriller, to be sure. You may remember that the Marlins won it in the eleventh inning. Dave's gratitude to the two men was unbounded; and, of course, he had to get them back to Cleveland before getting himself back to Philadelphia.

Near an I-95 North on-ramp, the three stopped to get gas; and– would you believe it!–standing at the gas station exit was a young man wearing an Indians cap and holding an Indians pennant, as well as a hand-painted sign that said "Cleveland or Bust."

"Get in!" they said, unanimously. "If you'll help drive, we'll each get a few extra minutes of sleep."

Shmini Atseres Hebrew. "The Eighth Day of the Assembly" holiday, Ashkenazic pronunciation
Simchas Torah Hebrew. "The Rejoicing of the Law" holiday, Ashkenazic pronunciation

Epistolary Communications

Dear Judah,

Reva and I have just had words accepted by *Wordnik,* the online neologisms dictionary. Mine is a verb, "occude," meaning "to suffer from Obsessive Compulsive Disorder." Reva's is "prccc," for "premature cognitive commitment," meaning "thoughts and actions of seniors that result in making them old before their time." Please don't worry whether we are suffering from these ailments. To our knowledge, we are not.

When my word was accepted, I associated it instantly with the reflexive voice of the Hebrew root "*Ayin Qof Dalet,*" "*l'hitaqed,*" intending a meaning of "to get bound up." I was so excited by my insight that I emailed a world-famous Israeli linguist, Belshazzar Daniel Illui, professor at the Hebrew University of Jerusalem.

Dear Professor Illui,

I feel very much humbled to be writing to you, like the "hyssop in the wall to a cedar of Lebanon." Also, I am conscious of the rabbinic proverb, "As is his name, so is he," because "*illui,*" as you know, means "prodigy" in Hebrew.

I am writing because I recently have had accepted by *Wordnik* the verb "occude" for "to suffer from Obsessive Compulsive Disorder" and I am struck by an uncanny parallel with the Hebrew root "*Ayin Qof Dalet.*" Do you think that I can get the support of Israeli linguists including yourself for proposing to the Hebrew Language Academy a new meaning of the root?

I would like to suggest also a new Hebrew noun for the ailment, "*aqedet.*"

Dear Dr. Levenson,

Thank you for your letter. You know, "cedar of Lebanon" strikes me as an "ivory-tower" metaphor; and I like to consider myself a "regular guy" and a "*mentsch.*" My last name "Illui" is an accident of birth. The real "*illui*" in our community of linguists is Gh'ilad Zuckermann, professor at the University of Adelaide in Australia. He has written about Hebrew as a "hybrid language" and is presently devoting himself to the revival of Australian indigenous, aboriginal, languages.

To address your interest in a new ramification of "*Ayin Qof Dalet*" my sense is that purists will insist that the root means, strictly, "binding with a rope." I do like the new English verb–"occude"–that you coined. It will be interesting to see whether it will "take" on your side of the Atlantic.

Dear Professor Illui,

I have just discovered on an academic website that the Hebrew Language Academy in 1994 coined the phrase "*niroza tirdonit kefiyatit*" for "Obsessive Compulsive Disorder." But I think that "*tirdonit*" (bothersome) and "*kefiyatit*" (coercive) are just as metaphorical as "binding with a rope." And besides "*aqedet*" is one word to the Language Academy's three, and it fits the disease-word pattern (*mishqal*).

Dear Dr. Levenson,

Understanding Professor Zuckermann's theories as I do, I feel certain that he won't support translating *the noun* for OCD into Hebrew, because the English (or German, or whatever) form should be maintained as an element of Hebrew's "hybridization." He might very much approve of your new meaning for the verb.

Dear Professor Illui,

I gladly accept what you have written. Accordingly, I think I'll save myself the trouble of making a proposal to the Language Academy. The authorities there, anyway, might well dismiss the suggestion of a layman out of hand.

But I'll tell you that I want to share with Professor Zuckermann my appreciation of his critical views about narrow-minded Hebraism. I suffered in my teens from over-zealous "all-Hebrew" instruction; and I sense that he will agree that indigenous Australians have been oppressed likewise by "all-English," just as Chicanos in California suffer from the "English-only" movement there.

Dear Dr. Levenson,

It's been a pleasure hearing from you. By all means, get in touch with Professor Zuckermann. You'll find him to be a very *simpático* guy.

Dear Judah,

Since I last wrote you, I've had three email exchanges with Professor Illui. I'm forwarding them to you. I think you'll enjoy reading them.

illui	Hebrew, Yiddish. "a prodigy," from the root *"Ayin Lamed He,"* meaning "ascend," as in *"Aliyah"* and *"maile," "mailes"*
mishqal	Hebrew. a "Hebrew form pattern"
niroza tirdonit kefiyatit	Hebrew. "a coercive, bothersome neurosis"

Prompt: "Write 300-500 words on ONE particularly unique joy, satisfaction, gripe, frustration, challenge, encounter, irony, learning, or growth, experienced in the Weisman Center Creative Writing Workshop."

"Save the Turtles"–a Joy

Esteemed listeners, I have had to fictionalize this piece, because rendering it as totally factual non-fictional reality would likely endanger my life. Several months ago a writing prompt here directed us to write an appeal to the wider community to contribute to a particular favorite charity. My charity was the National Save the Sea Turtle Foundation. In my appeal, I described the various services and benefits provided by the Foundation; and I listed the different levels of support contributors could choose. The $60-level promised the perquisites to the donor of a foam sea-turtle cushion and the adoption of a sea-turtle nest.

I wasn't actually soliciting money, just reading a sample appeal as a writing assignment; but participant Levinia Jeanne Wisewoman exclaimed, "Lead by example! Put your money where your mouth is! Don't just give such a measly a mount as $60!"

Well, I said to myself, *she's 100 per cent right*–and, as soon as class was over. I rushed home, wrote out a check for $180, ten times the lucky Jewish number of 18 (for "*Ḥai*"), and mailed it off.

Shortly thereafter I received a thank-you letter from the Foundation, which said that the officers had decided to give me a special reward for what they described was my particularly generous gift: they were assigning to me as *my* adoptive sea-turtle daughter the largest and most fertile turtle-egg producer along the hatcheries on the Fort Lauderdale beaches and they were according me the right to give her an English name. *That's a total non-brainer,* I thought, and I submitted as my name for such a wondrous sea turtle, "Levinia Jeanne."

I did pray to God that Levinia would be able to produce eggs without the need for any biological intervention on my part, fearing not only physical discomfort, not to say distress, for a particular part of my anatomy, but also, you better believe it, the grave sin of adultery (and I do mean "grave," meaning that's where I would wind up very quickly, no matter how enamored Reva is of certain reptiles, such as geckoes and, of course, tortoises.)

Boy, did Levinia come through. I received a "Certificate of Adoption" last week from the Foundation that Levinia laid a nest three and a half weeks ago on May 31st on a Fort Lauderdale beach and that "the nest will hatch within 45-55 days after the date laid." There is a photograph on the certificate of at least sixteen turtle hatchlings; but I am hoping that Lavinia's nest will contain eighteen, the lucky Jewish number that I mentioned. I understand that mother sea turtles often lay many more eggs than that.

The Foundation, furthermore, sent me a photograph of the triangular area of the sand in which the nest is partially buried and a sign with my name and an assigned number, to which a "Do Not Disturb Sea Turtle Nest" warning, as according to Florida state law, is stapled. I would propose a writing-group field trip to see the site, but I am loath that our group, numbering about 15 as it does, would disturb my precious babies.

This piece was in the "Humor" section of *EHAM*. Since it is semi-fictional, I am reprinting it in "Fiction" [in *GM*] here.

Sidney

Did you know that a group of geese is called a "gaggle" and that a group of ducks is called a "bevy"? For that matter, I might as well tell you now that, though the male goose is called a "gander," the female goose is simply a "goose" and that, though the male duck is called a "drake," the female duck is simply a "duck." Baby geese are "goslings," and baby ducks are "ducklings." "Hatchlings" are goslings or ducklings that have recently hatched. Popularly–and often by me also, for simplicity's sake–collectives of geese and ducks are just called "geese" and "ducks."

Be all these designations as they may, my wife Reva and I used to try to befriend the lone goose near Kings Point's Seville section in Delray Beach, Florida. It was mysterious in its exceptionality. We never knew whether it was male or female; and it never accompanied a spouse we could contrast it with–for the attempted determination of its gender. And so we gave it the unisex name of "Sidney."

Sidney no longer frequents Kings Point, and we wonder if any Kings Pointer knows where it has gone. If so, would you kindly inform us via the administrative office?

What was very striking was that it often seemed to be chaperoning ducks or egrets–either swimming in the pond, walking on the grass, or crossing the street. We sometimes saw it by itself looking for food in East End Cafe's parking lot. Fancying myself a modern-day Hugh Lofting character–Lofting pioneered the first of the many Dr. Dolittle series about people who learned to converse with birds and animals–I used to try to speak directly to and question Sidney. I especially wanted to know its feelings about the Kings Point ducks and how the relationship with them began.

The communication never got that far; but one night, in a dream, a mallard duck appeared to me. She began a conversation, "We hear that you want to learn about Sidney's past."

"Yes," I answered. "Who told you about me?"

"Well, all the mallards down here have learned through the grapevine that you grew up in Boston and loved Robert McCloskey's book *Make Way for Ducklings* about our northern matriarch and her eight ducklings Jack, Kack, Lack, Mack, Nack, Ouack, Pack, and Quack. She was my great-great-grandmother. Kack was my great-grandfather. He was the duck from our clan who made the big move of relocating to Florida."

"What's your name?

"Call me 'Tia Linda.'" I hear quacking all day and am happy that my name doesn't end in 'ack.'"

"Well, Tia Linda, do you know how Sidney got connected with ducks? Was it here at Kings Point? Did it associate with ducks from an early age? Was it male or female?"

"Indeed, it was at the beginning of its life. Yes, it was at Kings Point. Sidney's mother, whose name was Betty, after laying an egg, was taken away by a poacher to be slaughtered and eaten. She made such a row that the perpetrator didn't realize that he had left behind the egg, even though it was large. Her sister Amanda had had three eggs of her own removed from under her. She was very distraught; but, when she saw the goose egg, she hurried over and set on it until it hatched, as if it had been her own. Thus, the goose you call Sidney was with ducks from the moment of its hatching. We mallards are convinced that it preferred from the beginning to be with ducks because it actually thought that it *was* a duck!"

"Thank you ever so much, Tia Linda. But you didn't say whether Sidney was male or female."

"To tell you truth, we ourselves never knew what Sidney was; but that didn't matter to us in the slightest."

Reva and I hope that Sidney may have simply migrated north for the summer, perhaps to the Boston Public Garden to be with the northern duck relatives, and that we'll see it again in the fall. In lieu of getting more information about it at this time, on the strength of my conversation with Tia Linda in the dream, perhaps I would be advised to improve my bird-language skills and to try to become a Kings Point Dr. Dolittle.

(I wrote this story in response to a prompt to write about a situation ending with a person saying, "I can't believe I didn't see that coming.")

Silver Jewelry in Mexico

I am Señora Rosa Nuñez Grijalva. I teach Spanish to the visiting students in the School for International Training here in Oaxaca, Mexico; and I also, as do many of my colleagues, sell silver jewelry on the side. Silver is plentiful here in Southern Mexico because our area is one of the largest producers of silver in the world. It is now November of 2013, and this semester I have an unusual group of students in my Spanish class, four Americans and two Canadians. One American is more "unusual" than the other five students, and I will tell you one thing about him in a minute. His Mexican name is "Don Eduardo." Besides completing his course of studies here, he has wanted to buy silver jewelry from me to give as gifts. And so I invited him to my home to choose from the many items I have.

We sat down at the dining-room table, where I showed him, one by one, rings, bracelets, earrings, necklaces, and cufflinks. But he quickly lost patience with the progress of the display. I was quite surprised, for I had never experienced anyone so seemingly disinterested in my jewelry.

"Señora," he tried to reassure me, "believe me, I love the jewelry; but I prefer to see things in a panorama. I similarly don't enjoy a poet's reading a poem to me; I much prefer seeing a poem in a full-page spread where my eyes can move and make connections in all directions rapidly. Take me to your jewelry cabinet, open the drawers one by one, and let me see 40 pieces at a time in a visual sweep."

"You must be out of your mind," she replied. "I never show my pieces that way. Someone will rob me blind. I know you're honest, but you'll never get me to show you where my jewelry cabinet is."

With that, knowing that the quality of the goods was high and that he was getting a huge bargain, he simply said, "Señora, choose any three pairs of earrings and any five rings and tell me what I owe you."

Meanwhile, I learned that Don Eduardo was becoming captivated by Mexican tapestries.

Six months later, as he was getting ready to return to America, he made another appointment to come to my house and buy a second batch of jewelry. This time he bought three bracelets and three necklaces.

Saying goodbye, he said, "Señora, it's been an enormous pleasure doing business with you. I am concerned that you not think that I am a wealthy spendthrift. It's just that the merchandise is very beautiful and the prices are irresistible. The same goes for the tapestries I've been buying. I've bought 15."

I said to myself, "I can't believe I didn't see that coming!"

The Nazirite's Vow

(in deep appreciation to Meir Zev ("Volvie") Greenberger for his expert teaching and elucidation of *Masekhet* (Tractate) *Nazir)*

I, Itamar ben Berekhya HaKohen, have worked organizing schools in Judea under the leadership of *Kohen Gadol* (High Priest) Yehoshua ben Gamla at the beginning of the reign of the second King Agrippas in the year 3824 since the Creation of the World. As my readers know, Yehoshua ben Gamla was an extraordinary high priest, more principled than others at the time who paid lavishly for their appointments and who then took bribes for favors. Clearly, the Romans "set the tone," because Agrippas had to pay *them* off sufficiently to get his way in many matters and needed to recoup his expenses. But our rabbis knew that Agrippas was not an innocent either in his high-handed dealings, as in the deft pun that they whispered, "Beware of *'egrophah shel malkhut* (the fist of the kingship)." Sure enough, before the year was out, Agrippas replaced Yehoshua ben Gamla with Mattathias ben Theophilus. Though ben Gamla is out of office, he has continued in his educational leadership. It is now the year 3826 and the tensions in Jerusalem are becoming very difficult. Overall the Roman soldiers who help Agrippas "keep order" treat the population–Jewish and Idumaean–harshly. Fights among groups have been breaking out frequently, and the Romans arrest troublemakers and throw them into jail at will. I hear scuffles, in fact, outside the window of my small study right now.

"Zealots" have been fighting back against the Romans, and we even have "*kohanei hamiqdash*" (Sanctuary priests) joining them. But the "Zealots" have now gone so far as to depose Mattathias ben Theophilus and to choose a new high priest by lot–obviously to do their bidding–an ignorant rustic named Pinḥas ben Shmuel of the priestly family of Yakhin, which is not even one of the six priestly families from which high priests have been traditionally chosen. Yehoshua ben Gamla, *Kohen Gadol* two years ago, expressed that the future of the Jewish People depends on the *talmud Torah* (Torah study) of all, but especially of the young; and, sensing that he might not be allowed to keep his position for long, he undertook to do something truly important in the time in office he would be given. And what was that? He organized schools throughout Judea for Jewish boys five-years-old and older. What a wonderful idea!

He needed teachers, and he sent out a call for young men to accept service as teachers in all the schools. I don't need to tell you that the pay was small, but what he could promise was free room and board–and he got a satisfactory response. As in previous generations, the *mitzvah* of teaching Torah was the main motivation for our young people.

So many of the older generation say that "the young only care about themselves"–especially in these difficult times–but don't believe it! I had a role in setting up five small schools in the southeast corner of Jerusalem and finding teachers for them. I will never forget one young man who came to my small office outside of the *Beit Hamiqdash* (the Central Sanctuary) by the name of Ḥananiah ben Yirmiah.

We sat on rickety chairs in from of a small table. After brief introductions, I said, "Ḥananiah ben Yirmiah, I assume you're here because you know we're looking for teachers."

"*Adoni* (Mister) Itamar," he said, "That's correct. I'm eager to be a teacher for you and I can do a good job. But I have a particular need, which I want to explain to you."

"What is it, Ḥananiah? I'll try to be helpful."

"I'm engaged to be married, and I don't want my "*arusah*" (fiancée) to see me for three and a half months."

"Why is that?

"It's because I want to be a "*nazir l'me'ah yamim*" (a nazirite for 100 days)."

"Can you tell me if you have a particular reason for that? Not so many people undertake such a rigorous obligation."

I leaned forward in my chair to hear him better.

"The matter is this, and I hope and pray that you can put yourself in my place and try to understand me."

"Go on. You sound very sincere. It's not my business really, but if you want to tell me what's in your heart, I believe *Hashem* (God) wants me to listen to you."

"*Ba'avonotai harabim*" (because of my many sins), I was engaged twice before and each time the engagement got broken off. I've been devastated. "I want to appeal to *Hashem* this time with all my heart and soul that He recognize that I'm a good person and see me through to the *ḥuppah* (marriage canopy). My fiancée lives in a village 20 miles to the west. My reason for undertaking *nezirut* for 100 days is that I consider that a respectable minimum amount of time to devote to my holy purpose.

"I'll be particularly eager to come to Jerusalem because I want to keep my *nezirut* secret from my fiancée in case she will think that it's an attempt to "force *Hashem*" and that it'll have the opposite effect." Also, if I'm away for the duration of the *nezirut,* she won't know that I'm not drinking wine for *qiddush* and that I'm not cutting my beard and hair. I certainly will try not to invalidate my *nezirut* in the third way forbidden by the Torah, coming in contact with a dead body."

"You've made a most creditable impression on me, Ḥananiah. I will assign you to a school where I think you will appreciate both the children and the parents and vice versa."

Ḥananiah left for his school. One mother and father generously offered him a room in their home, and all the parents agreed to host him for meals on different evenings.

Ḥananiah's circumstances were pleasant.

The days turned into weeks and the weeks, into months. Soon it was the beginning of the fourth month, the 94th day of Ḥananiah's *nezirut*. Three days passed, and on the 97th day a terrible thing happened. A brawl arose in front of the school. A Jew and an Idumaean got into a fight. A Roman soldier intervened on the side of the Idumaean and tried to separate the combatants, but the Idumaean was not to be restrained and tried to lunge past the Roman at the Jew.

Ḥananiah went outside to try to prevent the fight from spilling into the school. The Jew stepped four feet backwards, and Ḥananiah found himself between him, on the one hand, and both the Roman and the Idumean, on the other. The Idumean, wanting to keep fighting, pressed forward and inadvertently bumped the Roman hard. Enraged, the Roman wheeled around, drew his sword and plunged it deep into his heart. He died instantly and fell forward onto Ḥananiah.

Ḥananiah thus became a "*t'me met*" (impure by virtue of contact with a dead body) and his *nezirut* was automatically invalidated. What a disappointment after 97 days of his great self-discipline!

All of the *kohanim* (priests) of the Sanctuary and all the teachers in Yehoshua ben Gamla's network of schools learned very quickly what had happened, and our hearts went out to Ḥananiah. We invited him to a meeting to try to cheer him up.

You might have thought that our purpose was something like "*niḥum avelim*" (comforting mourners), but that wasn't the case at all. Former *Kohen Gadol* Yehoshua ben Gamla, ten top-ranked *kohanim,* and ten rabbis of the Sanhedrin came as well. Yehoshua ben Gamla spoke in the name of the assembled, as follows:

"Ḥananiah, all of us here admire you greatly for your piety. You have set a remarkable example for all the young people of Jerusalem, and, in fact, of the whole of Judea and beyond. You, of course, know that your *nezirut* is "*soter*" (forfeited); but we want to urge you to accept that fact and complete a new cycle of 100 days properly. All of the elders and leaders here will also undertake a one-day fast each and pray to *Hashem* on your behalf.

"Immediately upon the completion of our individual fasts we intend to send a delegation to your fiancée and her family to inform them what a truly wonderful *ḥatan* (groom) they have and that we want to make the wedding *here in Jerusalem* as soon as possible.

"We'll explain that we consider that your *nezirut* has been an inspiration for all of us. We expect that your *kallah* (bride) will have no trouble accepting your growing long hair and abstaining from wine until the second *nezirut* cycle is completed. You, of course, will need no reminders to try to 'keep yourself out of harm's way.'"

The wedding took place four months later in a precinct of the *Beit Hamiqdash.* There wasn't a dry eye there during the recitation of the wedding blessings. We feasted and recited *birkat hamazon* (grace after meals), and the men and women danced in separate circles. All in attendance rejoiced heartily for the couple. We were deeply proud of Ḥananiah–no one more than the *kallah.*

"Trial by Fire": Joe's First Four Months in the District

It was September 1996. Joe was new to the School District of Philadelphia. He had taught in private school settings in different regions of the country and had heard that inner-city schools with populations of "at-risk" students would be a challenge. He had moved to "The City That Loves You Back" (the gender-neutral version of "The City of Brotherly Love") for family reasons, and he had a bit of confidence that his rapport-building skills would help him succeed with students; but, to be sure, he had his share of apprehension about what awaited him. He was not to be disappointed that his first year of teaching in Philadelphia would be interesting–in the full sense of the Chinese proverbial blessing "May you live in uninteresting times!"

Joe's overriding need was survival. Receiving stimulation, fulfillment, approval, gratitude, and praise was completely secondary for him to his just making it through the year.

A new Master Curriculum Plan was rolled out that year; and he had no way of knowing that the theme that all teachers had to orient instruction around–"What Is Justice?"–would be changed the following year.

A mischievous kid nearly killed Joe in class the third week of September. You may think that's an exaggeration. It is perhaps, but only a little. What happened was this. It was before computers were widely used for classroom instruction, and Joe projected hand-printed text with an overhead projector onto a screen. The screen was suspended in front of the chalkboard from two hooks that extended six inches from the upper part of the front wall. It happened that the screen was two-thirds of its length down, and its position disturbed student James' aesthetic sensibilities: he wanted it either all-the-way down or all-the-way up. But Joe needed it just where it was. If it had been all the way down, it would have blocked the chalkboard; and if it had been all the way up, Joe would have had to struggle to reach up and pull it down.

Joe did not sit at his desk routinely; but, when taking attendance one morning, he had to, in order to concentrate on some details. While he was doing so, James snuck around the desk, pulled the screen down a bit to release the spring, and then started to ease the screen upwards with both hands. But the screen escaped him, flew out of his hands, and zoomed up so fast that its cylindrical housing became unhooked from its fastening on the right side. Secured on the left side, it swung down in a circular arc with great force and missed Joe's head with only inches to spare. It was a close call! How did Joe feel about it? Strange as it may seem, his main emotion was relief that he had survived another day.

Later that month James attempted to put his noseprint on the overhead-projector film. I know that individuals don't have personal-specific noseprints. James' nose would simply have left a magic-marker smudge on a word. Not wanting him to do so or to crinkle the film, Joe blocked his right cheek gently with his left hand and prevented James' head from getting under the lamp and his nose from touching the film.

"You hit me!" James exclaimed. "I'm going to the principal."

Taking out a discipline report called a "pink slip," Joe said, "James, if you're going to the principal, I have to write you up."

"Do what you gotta do!"

And so, during his free period Joe brought a pink slip on James to the principal, including in the report that James falsely accused him of hitting him. Hitting a student being a grave offense, the principal summoned both James and Joe to her office the following morning.

She asked James, "Do you admit that you tried to put a noseprint on the overhead-projector film?"

"Yes, but it was only a joke. Obviously. The teacher shouldn't have hit me!"

The situation was so ludicrous and James had such a long history of mischief–besides having been ordered by the police to wear an ankle bracelet tracking his movements–that the principal believed Joe's side of the story completely. "C'mon James," she ruled. "The teacher was trying to protect his projector. Go back to class, and stop doing stupid stuff."

In truth, Joe learned a very important lesson from the episode. A teacher at all costs must never so much as *touch* a student. The most fleeting touch can be misinterpreted.

Well, the reverse ought to be the case also; and it *was* theoretically– but, as Joe learned in October, the burden was put on *teachers* not to be *in the vicinity of* a shove or a punch. The watchword was "Keep yourself out of harm's way!" District schools at that time had begun to put beefed-up security in buildings; and, in one Professional-Development afternoon, the chief of the security guards addressed faculty and staff about new protocols. At the conclusion of his talk, he exclaimed, "For goodness sake, if a student starts to walk out of class five minutes early, don't block his or her way. Let the student leave, and deal with the infraction afterwards."

Ironically, the principal the day before had demanded that teachers monitor exits from class carefully. The corridors had been filling up with students before the bell rang.

Joe hoped that his sense of humor might rescue him in tough situations, and so it did a week later. He was standing at the door in order to discourage students from leaving class early. That position worked generally, but not in the case of a young man–named Fred–who attempted to walk "through him"–almost literally. The student, with a sweeping sideways motion of both arms, exclaimed, "Out of my way, pussy!"

With all due respect, female readers must not underestimate the rage in a man that that insult can provoke. And it did in Joe's case, but he had the innate good sense to know that he needed to "defuse the situation." And so he very calmly responded, "Why are you insulting your mother?"

Fred countered, "I'm not insulting my mother; I'm insulting *you!*"

But Joe had caught his attention, and Fred paused and asked, "Why did you say that?"

Joe recognized immediately that Fred had given him a "ridiculous-to-sublime" *teaching moment*, and he said, "You know, Fred, you just spoke poetry. You used a brilliant metaphor, a poetic comparison without the preposition 'like.'"

At this point, every single student, especially the young women, sat in rapt attention.

Joe continued, "'Pussy' is a girl-word."

"No it isn't," Fred interrupted, "it means 'cat.'"

"Don't play me, Fred–not the way you used it, it doesn't! 'Pussy' is a very special female part, as you well know. When you called me that, you were using the word as a metaphor, a poetic comparison, as I said. You were calling me 'a girl,' and you meant the comparison negatively. As such you were not only insulting your mother; you were insulting every young woman in the class."

"You expect me to believe that?" he tried to defend himself. "The girls themselves use that insult against boys, and even against other girls."

"Well, that's because they're trying to fit into the school's dominant male culture, as expressed in the T-shirt slogan 'Bitch and Proud of It.' 'Bitch' is a negative stereotype also. But the bell is about to ring, and that's enough of an English lesson for today."

With that the bell did ring. Joe extended his hand. Fred, to Joe's amazement, reciprocated, and they shook hands cordially. "See you tomorrow, Fred. Have a nice day!"

"You too!"

In the second week of November, another double entendre took pride of place, but this time it occurred with a Spanish word that Joe coined spontaneously, not ever having heard it before. It happened in an exchange with Juan, a 13-year-old student newly arrived from Ecuador. Every morning Juan refused to push his hood back. Joe tried a different approach for days in succession in his attempts to enforce Juan's compliance with the District's no-hat policy.

Sweatshirts with hoods, "hoodies," strictly speaking, were not allowed in the first place, but Joe considered that rule unenforceable. The main thing, at any rate, was "not to confront–give the direction and move on."

On the first day of the back-and-forth, Joe stated the rule to Juan. He pointed to the hood the day after. The day after that he simply said, "The hood!" Juan shooed him off with his right hand. On the fourth day Joe said, "Juan, if the principal walks in and sees your hood, I'm in trouble."

Juan replied, "That's your problem!"

Joe thought on the fifth day that he might subsequently have better luck in Spanish; and so, finding the word for "hood" in the dictionary, he tried, "*La capucha!*"–but to no avail.

Next came Joe's *tour de force.* It was the sixth day. He looked at Juan, hooded as ever; and, from deep in his unconscious, he uttered, "*Capuchito!!!*"

Juan was stunned. With eyes blazing, he raised his voice, "Don't call me that!"

Joe hadn't expected any reaction from Juan at all, but he realized on the spot that Juan might have given him a new opportunity; and so he had. He said, "Of course, Juan, I won't call you that again, but you have to take your hood off."

And Juan did, shaking his fist and exclaiming, "Don't call me that ever again!"

To everyone's surprise, when his hood was off, out flowed a beautiful head of long black hair over a newly visible handsome face. The girl to his right was so taken that she jumped up, put her arms around his head, and exclaimed, "*Mira, está guapo!*" (Look, he's handsome!)

Juan, embarrassed, squirmed from under her arms and sunk lower in his seat.

The next day he was not in class; and, then, he was absent for two whole weeks. Joe grew concerned, worrying that he might have precipitated some kind of emotional breakdown.

But, in truth, Juan had simply gone on a trip to Ecuador. Lo and behold, first thing in the morning of the Monday of the third week, three students came rushing into Joe's room saying, "Teacher, *capuchito* is back!"

At the beginning of class a period later, Juan took his seat and upbraided Joe sharply, "I told you not to call me that."

Joe had to protest to him that he hadn't, for it was all his friends' doing.

Why did the word upset Juan so much? A Spanish-speaking colleague suggested that he might have interpreted the word not as "little boy with the hood," but as "little boy from where they wear hoods," "hoodies" being a socioeconomic mark of identification. Another colleague, on the other hand, offered the analysis that Juan thought Joe said "*capullito*," (with two "*ll*"s), attempting to pronounce the two "*ll*'s as "*zh*" in "*capuzhito.*" "*Capullo*" means "bud," and "*capullito*" would mean "little bud." The 275,000-word *Oxford Spanish Dictionary,* in fact, suggests the very vulgar colloquial metaphorical meaning, "Little dickhead!"

Joe later recognized that Juan most certainly had taken the word as a vicious gay slur, not realizing that it had been completely unintentional, Joe not having even known the meaning of "*capucha*" in October.

December was a month of fireworks. In the first week, Joe stayed at his desk at dismissal time to mark papers before going home. He left the classroom door open. Suddenly a student rushed into the room and threw a lit firecracker directly at him. It exploded in midair three feet from Joe's right ear. Experiencing a continuous ringing, Joe went immediately to an ear specialist to find out whether his tympanum had been ruptured. The doctor found no physical damage, but did administer a hearing test, which revealed minor hearing loss that he said probably had been preexistent and longstanding.

Why did the student throw the firecracker? By chance, Joe met a young woman friend of his a few months later in the supermarket. She revealed very empathetically that the young men in her group had been playing an ongoing "Truth or Dare" game. That explained the firecracker mystery and also why another young man in November had rushed into Joe's room and–inexplicably, as it had seemed–lifted a leg onto Joe's desk and swept all of Joe's papers and books onto the floor with it.

From a firecracker to full-fledged arson the following week, planned very carefully by a disturbed student. At the beginning of the next-to-the-last period of a day, the student very politely asked Joe for a pass to the office timed 25 minutes hence. Then he took his seat in the back of the room in front of the radiators which extended along the back wall. A long rectangular metal box covered them. Inside was a month-long accumulation of balled-up sheets of paper discarded by students who hadn't wanted to wait until class ended to use the wastebasket.

The student quietly doused lighter fluid onto the paper the length of the radiators. About five minutes before he was to use his pass, he threw a few lit matches inside. His calculation was sharp. It took ten minutes for the fire to start, but by then he was gone.

A fire blazed. The entire school needed to be evacuated, and the fire received city-wide publicity on radio station KYW. An in-school investigation ensued, and every single student in the class was questioned by security guards. Joe was absolved from all blame, because, as a number of students testified, "The teacher was alert in class. He had smelled lighter fluid and said a number of times, 'Anyone lighting a cigarette will get a pink slip.'"

A few students, to be sure, identified the perpetrator, whose pyrotechnics, in fact, continued. A few days later he was caught lighting a fire in a wastebasket of the main office. It struck Joe as a classic case of a "cry for help," but that wasn't much consolation, for the consequences for him from the charge of negligence could have been dire. Colleagues, though, approached Joe in subsequent days,

"Congratulations, you've survived your first fire!" Joe then realized grimly that the setting of fires in schools was not totally uncommon.

By January Joe was saying to himself, "If I got through September to December as a teacher in the District, I'll be able to survive anything!" The next year he had increased confidence and was, in fact, a significant source of strength to several colleagues.

MEMOIRS

A Knock at the Door

Law enforcement officials warn of the great need to exercise care in responding to a knock on the door. At a minimum one should turn on the outside lights at night. It may even be advisable, one offered, to call 9-1-1.

I, at any rate, have two stories about knocks on doors and want to relate one of them now. The first is my proactive one of needing to hear the knock in the first place.

The chimes in my house in Philadelphia were defective. They simply did not work.

Because of my subpar hearing, furthermore, and also the distance of the front door from the dining room and the kitchen–the living room and foyer being in between–and the fact that the front door had thick wood, which muffled sound, I often didn't hear that someone had been knocking.

I took a five-day vacation in Dublin in August of 2010 with my son Judah and daughter Aliza. Knowing that Ireland is famous for iron products, I had researched companies that produced door knockers and I located a specialty score near Trinity College, called Knobs and Knockers. Besides scores of knockers, it carried hundreds of door knobs. The knockers came in two basic designs: a one-piece base with the knocking part swinging down against its bottom, or a two-piece set with a separate small round ball to be affixed separately below the top part for the knocking part to strike against. I bought the second type. On the top part were engraved the head and flowing mane of a strong, protective lion.

The store owner got for me from his stock a box according to the code number of the respective item on display on the wall of the store; and when I opened the box in the hotel that evening, the bottom small ball was missing. I knew I needed to get the mistake rectified the following morning.

I used to go to sleep at 10 p. m., and Judah and Aliza on a few of the evenings went out "on the town" on their own. That particular evening they had some excitement. They witnessed police chasing a thief from the nightspots northward towards the Liffey River. Instead of surrendering, the thief jumped over the railing into the river, whereupon the pursuit turned into a rescue operation. I awakened at 2 a.m. from the excited conversation of my kids as they returned to the hotel room and wanted to tell me about their adventure.

But since they needed to sleep late in the morning, I left for the Knobs and Knockers store at 8:45 a.m. before they woke up. The store was not to open until 9, but the owner, who had arrived earlier than I, let me in. I told him what the problem was and he said, "I'll have to get a replacement set for you from the basement. Stay here. I'm putting you in charge. Don't let anyone into the store."

While he was downstairs, however, an elderly woman knocked on the glass door. It was a chilly August morning; she was shivering; she thought I had authority; and she was insistent that I let her in even though it was still, technically, before hours. I did so, reluctantly, nervous that the owner would take me to task about it.

On the contrary. He assessed the situation and said, with overstatement– characteristically British, but here Irish, "So you made an executive decision, did you?"

Prompt: "Upon awakening you jump out of bed. A voice you had heard said, 'Step into your door mirror.' What happened next? Write a story of 300 to 500 words."

Note: This version of the piece "A Voice I Had Heard Before Awakening" was read on April 30th, 2018, at the Creative Writing Workshop in the Weisman Center in Delray Beach, Florida.

A Voice I Had Heard
Before Awakening

Every now and then I wake up abruptly in the morning at the end of an extraordinarily dynamic and symbolically rich dream that I don't fully understand and I rush first to the door mirror to see if I am still me, then to my computer to record as much of the dream as I can, and then back to the door mirror where I gaze at my reflection while trying to fathom the dream's message. I stare so intently at the mirror that I feel as if I am "entering" it. More on this in a minute.

That very thing happened, believe it or not, last Monday afternoon when after an apology to Jeanne for having misunderstood something she had said in class and after a longer-than-anticipated conversation in the parking lot with Barbara, the author of the admittedly magnificent prompt for today, I went home, processed thoughts with Reva, and took an afternoon nap–at the end of which I had a frightening "afternoonmare" and awakened in a cold sweat. It had been about a struggle with an arbitrary and inflexible authority figure.

I stood before the door mirror pondering and re-pondering the meaning of the dream.

Metaphorically speaking, the mirror for me ceases to reflect back, but invites me through it to a new dimension of existence in which the obscure becomes clear. And so it was last Monday.

As a writer whose passion is the most correct word and the most apt image possible–and impeccable logic as far as validity, sequence, and truth go–I labor over and over again in my mind to ascertain improvements for the above–especially when something relating to me has been expressed. Sure enough I entered and emerged from the mirror with an astounding new grasp of five interrelated agonies in my unconscious.

Here they are:

1. Of course I understood that class members' praise of my piece "I Won't Contest the Divorce" was well-meaning. I believed, though, that the assertion that "it was my best piece ever" was an invidious comparison with earlier pieces I had written. I explained this last Monday in the "Ten-Minute Writing."

2. I recalled on the spot the leader of a 2014 group praising a piece of a participant that it had been "the best piece written that day" and my instant protest, "We are not in competition with each other here!"

3. I recalled an opinion expressed in even another writing group, pressed forcefully, that prompts should not be quoted at the beginning of a piece. I differed in not minding at all indication of the source of my inspiration, as in the case of (the written version of) this piece.

4. I recalled editorializing of critiquers in a writing group that some of my stuff was too difficult to understand and/or was irrelevant and should, therefore, be cut. I considered those comments as "crossing the boundary of legitimate critiquing."

The leader, in fact, had no idea of the importance to me of two particular paragraphs which meant nothing to her. They were not difficult to understand at all; that was an evasion on her part.

5.   Last but not least, I recalled a company's unutilizable review of my first book, for which I had paid $450–which was riddled with inaccuracies, falsehoods, and bias–and, especially the assertion in it that my "'Memoirs' section was 'the book's stongest.'" Thinking unexpressible bitter execrations re the matter, I considered an utter travesty the company's justification of the reviewer's subjective views as "opinion-based analysis," an outrageous contradiction in terms. My subsequent fictional satire of "Gornishthelfen Laughables. com" (Yiddish for "nothing helps") lambasts that particular company–effectively, I trust.

I have genuine concerns relating to the need for the striving for truth in writers' groups. I feel I have been terribly misunderstood a number of times in this one. I insist strenuously, screaming voicelessly to the Heavens, that, as God is my witness, I have not been governed by irrational unconscious motivations to be antagonistic and disruptive.

Respectfully offered,
Yours truly,
Eddie L.

Experiences in Camping

I love camping in a tent and the accompanying activities of cooking on a Coleman stove and sitting around the campfire. From one's campsite base, one can venture into the neighboring countryside, climb mountains, and enjoy sailing or canoeing. My children and I have camped up and down the Eastern Seaboard and in Maine, New Hampshire, and Upstate New York. Our most spectacular places have been Acadia National Park in Maine and Great Smoky National Park in North Carolina/Tennessee. Camping is our happiest way of experiencing nature and America's natural beauty directly.

My camping vacations with my children have generally been unmarred by accidents, although once a 20-foot tree branch dropped on our site when we were away and another time the steep rocks of Mount Monadnock in New Hampshire evoked fear of broken bones and sprains.

To be sure, the bear outside of my tent in Yosemite National Park in California–before my children were born–has never receded far from mind.

Real danger, however, occurred in New Hampshire in August 2001 when my daughter Aliza and I capsized our canoe because of brisk winds, a strong lake current, and careless uncoordinated shifting of our weight. I labored strenuously–in vain–to empty the canoe of water by turning it over and over; I later learned that the only way to do that is to jump on the stern and make the canoe project perpendicularly upward. All the while people in a cabin cruiser 250 yards away were watching us and were thinking that we were playing.

After ten minutes, I said to Aliza, "We have no choice; we have to let the canoe go and do the backstroke [because it is the stroke that requires the least energy] to the island over there [150 yards in the other direction from the shore]!"

"Ee, it has leeches!" as she had heard.

Ironically, once we let the canoe go, the people in the boat realized that we had not been playing and came to rescue us. Aliza and I were very fortunate, for our life preservers were old and waterlogged and could have done us more harm than good.

Three weeks after our return home 9/11 occurred. On September 15th in my local Pathmark supermarket the cashiers were collecting contributions to the national relief effort. I wrote out a $100 check, more than I would have given ordinarily, in gratitude to God and in honor of our rescuers.

I Was a Catholic Educator

My title, with the word "was," might strike some of my Catholic friends as an impossibility, in the sense that "once a Catholic always a Catholic," as I have heard expressed. Except that in my case it is the complete truth because I am Jewish and, for that matter, have always been Jewish. I was really, however, a "Catholic educator" (in quotation marks, to be sure) from 1980 to 1995, when I taught Religion for eight years at Villanova University (in its Department of Theology, no less) and then Latin for eight years in two Indiana Catholic high schools, at St. Joseph's High School in South Bend and at Marian High School in Mishawaka. For the latter period, I was a member of the National Catholic Educators Association. When I left the Midwest in 1995, my St. Joseph's colleagues presented me with the school's polo shirt and dubbed me an "honorary Catholic."

And not only that. In 1994-1995, I was St. Joseph's faculty representative to the "Bishop's Council." Therein is a story. The teachers had a union; and being Jewish, I felt that it was "in my blood" to become an active member. The negotiations with the double diocese of Fort Wayne-South Bend became tense, and the teachers began to plan a "radical" one-day strike with picketing and a whole eight-hour bit. But, at the last moment, the Bishop decided he could not continue in the process and abruptly withdrew his recognition of us. No further movement was possible, for he had effectively "broken" the union. He, however, created in its place a "Bishop's Council" for the discussion of issues and promulgation of plans–for the four high schools in the double diocese.

There was need for one faculty representative to the Council from each of the four schools. In some cases, I think, individual principals appointed one. In others, there were elections, as was the case in my South Bend school, St. Joseph's. Our principal announced that she wanted to hold an election, but a problem emerged in that not a single teacher expressed willingness to run. I found myself experiencing Catholic politics first-hand from within. The principal chose to put the complete list of teachers up on the bulletin board in the faculty mailroom and directed that teachers not wishing to run should cross their names off the list. 45 out of 50 teachers did.

I did not cross my name off because of one consideration, the criterion of a teacher's "service" to one's school. Three criteria were involved in rating a teacher: good teaching, extracurricular activities, and service. I had a particular problem with the latter, because I was teaching in two schools and considered that any service I would perform for one school would detract from, not contribute to, service in the other. So I reasoned that, though I had "no more chance of a snowball in Hell," in my father's words, to win the election, I wouldn't cross my name off the list, because if by the extremely remote chance I *would* win, my problem would be solved: I would be doing service directly for South Bend St. Joseph's and indirectly for Mishawaka Marian.

Well, I think God had an inscrutable design for me: I won the election. I attribute two reasons for the victory, one positive and one, perhaps, less so. First, I got along well with my colleagues; but, secondly, I think there may have been a sentiment of "Let's give the Bishop 'the Jewish guy.'" I duly attended the four Council meetings that school year and took very detailed minutes, which I distributed at St. Joseph's. I received compliments for them consistently that they were informative and well-written.

As well as Catholic politics, I experienced civic politics. I learned that there was an element of "town-gown" tension between the inhabitants of South Bend and Mishawaka and between the University of Notre Dame. This included a wider range of "townies" than one might have expected. The University has established for itself a separate "city," Notre Dame, Indiana, with its own zip code and post office, seceding, as it were, from South Bend. Many South Benders resented that. Also, in my schools there was anger that the University, in its goal of geographic diversity, accepted students from far and wide and didn't have room left for excellent locals.

I was aware that Mishawaka, a suburb, occupied a socioeconomic niche above that of South Bend. My respective students in combined Junior Classical League outings got along well with each other. A joke, however, told me by an elder of the South Bend Jewish community may have reflected tension between South Bend and Mishawaka *Jews.* He related that 50 years earlier a South Bend Catholic had stated to him that there wouldn't be any problem between Catholics and Jews "if the Jews had not killed Christ." He replied that he had answered, "It wasn't us! It was the Jews of Mishawaka!"

In my teaching at the two schools, I learned some important lessons about discipline, especially that whatever the limits are teenagers will test them. Some things happened that, had they been featured in a Hollywood film, viewers would have said they were completely unrealistic. For example, in the smaller Mishawaka school, which had only two floors, a young man climbed into the rafters between each one, with a water pistol in hand; crawled on top of classrooms; lifted up ceiling panels; and squirted water down, as best as he was able, into young women's cleavages. His male friends were aware all the while of his antics and became apoplectic with laughter.

On a personal note, I remember warmly all my friends in the two schools, especially the principals under whom I had the privilege to work. Four experiences with students stand out for me. One was with St. Joseph's students; three were with Marian's. A brother and sister were in different Latin classes of mine at St. Joseph's. They lived on a farm to the west of South Bend. They invited me and three of my children on a memorable hayride on a Sunday afternoon.

I had taught World Religions at Villanova; and, as such, I considered History of Religion, Comparative Religion, and Religious Symbolism to be important. In a Marian class once during the Easter and Passover seasons, students asked me about the Passover Seder ritual. I, therefore, brought into class *matzah,* parsley, and pieces of *maror,* bitter herb. Taken straight and getting into the sinuses via the back of one's tongue and nose, bitter herb can be devastating.

Not as a rule, but sometimes. And so it was in one student's case. I never anticipated that this would happen, but his first bite of a piece nearly knocked him out. Many times afterwards I had an anxious moment thinking that I could be accused of having brought a "foreign substance" into the classroom.

An unbelievable thing happened in the same class. Once I stupidly said to a student that, if he gave me the correct answer to a difficult question, I would stand on my head. I didn't notice that a friend whispered to him what to say. Then the class demanded that I fulfill my part of the bargain. I had no choice. All the students crowded around me and helped me get upside-down. Two students on each side held each of my legs up firmly. Remarkably, one student captured the moment in a photograph. It looks as if I was laughing, but that wasn't so. I was in distress, and the minute I got back on my feet I developed a nosebleed.

Finally, once at Thursday morning mass at Marian a guest priest presided. He prefaced the offering of the bread and the wine with an explanation that, though some Protestant students at the school, as he was aware, had expressed interest in receiving the sacrament, it was simply "against the rules." But, on the other hand, he encouraged non-Catholic students to come forward at the end and "receive a blessing." When the time came for that, several of my students nudged me on each shoulder, urging me, "Go up, Doc, get a blessing, get a blessing!" I smiled and politely declined to do so on the grounds that my religion is different. But, from a broader perspective, my years of teaching at St. Joseph's and at Marian were indeed blessings eight-fold.

I Was a Catholic Educator–Addendum

In the main part of this essay in *EHAM,* I lauded my "positive fit" as a Jewish teacher in Catholic-school settings in South Bend and Mishawaka, Indiana. Readers may recall my relating that a visiting priest at a mass explained that it was against the rules for Protestant students to receive communion, but that he encouraged them to "come up and get a blessing," whereupon my students nudged me on my shoulders, "Go on up, Doc, and get a blessing." I noted that, though my having a different religion made it awkward for me to receive the priest's blessing, my eight years of teaching in the diocesan schools of South Bend and Mishawaka, Indiana, were a blessing many times over.

For the sake of necessary balance, I want to add that all was not "peaches and cream" for me in my eight years of teaching in the Catholic schools. For that matter, it is true that it never was nirvana either for me teaching in Jewish educational settings in Boston and Philadelphia, at the University of Wisconsin, or in my 17 years in the School District of Philadelphia.

Two stressful experiences stand out for me in my teaching in Indiana. The first was in the context of the vigorous pro-life environment of the Catholic high school in which students and faculty participated in vigils and rallies for the cause. One student, with whom I incidentally got along exceptionally well, who was the son of a Notre Dame professor who was very close with a Notre Dame colleague who was one of the staunchest pro-life proponents on campus, asked me one morning in class whether I was pro-life or pro-choice. He must have sensed that Jews are generally more pro-choice than Catholics, and he wanted my opinion. He put me on the spot, but I felt I owed him a sincere from-the-heart answer.

In a Jewish way, I answered his question with a question, framing an issue very starkly, "Imagine a small-framed petite eleven-year-old girl who had been raped by her uncle and had gotten pregnant. Should such a young person be compelled to undergo the dangers of a life-threatening childbirth to bear a child of incest?"

The student answered, "Yes."

I continued, "What then would happen to both the child and the mother?"

He replied, "God will take care of them both."

I was much humbled in experiencing his deep faith; and, to this day, I am uncomfortable in reliving that brief dialogue, for I, in attempting to maintain a genuine relationship with the student, found myself–albeit under pressure–challenging the authority of the Catholic Church, which was my employer at the time.

The other major stress involved two students, a sister and a brother, in Latin 1 and Latin 2, respectively, with whom I had a more ambivalent relationship, because I had once caught them red-handed, each of them separately, cheating with crib sheets in tests. They were excellent students and they hardly needed to cheat; but, as I later learned from a friend of the brother, theirs were acts of bravado, according to which they wanted to "show me up" and demonstrate to their friends that it was "easy to cheat off of me." Well, I caught them; and they retaliated by going home and telling their mother that I had falsely accused them.

A few weeks later an incident in the Israeli-Palestinian conflict relating to the settlements was in the news. A student asked me a question about the "occupied territories," and I responded that I preferred the Israeli term "disputed territories," whereupon the brother blurted out loudly, "The Jews stole the Arabs' land!"

Stung, I replied that that sounded like an Anti-Semitic statement to me.

Shortly thereafter I was "on the carpet" in the office of the principal; she questioned me sharply whether I had or had not called [the student] a bigot.

I myself don't hold grudges. Later in the year the brother became quite seriously ill from an incorrect medicine and had to be hospitalized, whereupon I sent him a get-well card. I happened to meet the mother at a school event afterwards, and she was better-disposed to me than previously.

I Was a Thief

I was nine years old. What I did once was more than an indiscretion and less than a crime. I neither faced the conscquences nor made amends–to humans–for the act. I concealed it before "my fellow person," but not before God. It was a sin, the violation of the Eighth Commandment, "Thou Shalt Not Steal." I underestimated its seriousness in the development of my karma, but its effects played out powerfully in my unconscious and changed my life decisively.

I had a collection of national-flag cards, obtained in the purchase of small and flat Parade-brand bubble-gum rectangles. The possible card total was 100, and I had 98. One Sunday afternoon I visited the house of a third-grade classmate, I'll call him Teddy–an acquaintance, not a close friend. On a cluttered table in his room lay one solitary card, the flag of Norway. It was not a "rare" one, like that of what was then called "Irish Free State." I already had a Norway flag, but thinking I could use the duplicate for trading, I stole the card.

The next day when I came home from school, a somber scene greeted me. My brother Rob had gotten home before me and, having done something wrong in school that I had no way of knowing anything about, had been severely reprimanded by our mother. He was downcast, and he wasn't able to look me in the eye. The situation was incomprehensible to me. Had I been older, I might have been able to recognize in our mother's manner that something unfavorable to *me* had happened–for I, the older brother, as I look back, used to get into trouble and be criticized for things more than Rob. That afternoon it was Rob who was in the "hot seat."

Rob had taken my prized card collection and lost most of it in school–perhaps in a flipping-against-the-wall competitive game. Mother broke the news to me, let it sink in, and waited for me to respond.

I–to her and Rob's complete and utter surprise–reacted without anger or frustration, but with ready, resigned acceptance. For me, it was a matter of God's instant and overwhelming retribution for my having stolen the card! My sin was as great as King David's having Uriah the Hittite killed so he could marry Uriah's wife Bathsheba. The flag card I stole was "the poor man's lamb," as the prophet Nathan charged in his famous parable in chapter 12 of 2 Samuel. "*I* was the man who stole the lamb!"

The event was a turning point of my development. It precipitated a "conversion" (in the general technical sense) on my part culminating five years later in intense Orthodox observance and punctiliousness–a new foundation of my life, albeit the basis of the severe inner religious conflicts I was to suffer subsequently.

My Father, His Cats, and *Moby Dick*
by son Ben

May 2013. My father has four cats: Amber, Grise, Daggoo, and Tashtego. He got them five years ago when a friend suggested to him that cats were good companions and he had just finished reading Melville's *Moby Dick.* He talked of his ability to communicate with them and called my sister to tell her that she had some new sisters who would be competing with her in the family.

Tashtego

I never understood his fascination with *Moby Dick.* I had not opened the book until four months ago and I thought the cats were just another of his idiosyncrasies.

I remember the letters that would come in the mail from my Dad's lawyers and the long car rides between Philadelphia and New Jersey for weekend visits every month. Through these episodes I got to know him in spurts. I knew that he enjoyed laughing at his own jokes about George Washington's wooden teeth and was bemused by his mistaken attempts to speak Arabic to Hindu gas-station attendants. He was very good at Scrabble; and, as he described it, he has an evolutionary impulse to never turn back while driving. He's the creature who "needs to see what's over the next hill." He loved diners and his Australian "boonie cap," a camouflage bucket hat that he wore on all our hiking trips.

He never talked much about himself and his past. He would mention his father's criticisms, "Oh how my father would say, 'EDWARD, book learning isn't everything. You have to have plain common sense!'" and complain about my mother–"Your mother would give me hell about chewing with my mouth open." But then he'd chuckle and quickly change the subject.

I traveled with my brother and sister several times to help him organize and clean his house. Yet he refused to throw anything away and he continued to live with a year's worth of newspapers on his kitchen table. I couldn't see the floor of his house because orange medicine bottles, breath mints, and CD jewel boxes littered the carpet.

I decided to take a course at Princeton about *Moby Dick* and I didn't know it at the time, but my main motivation was to connect with him.

Even during that semester we didn't speak much about the book. Our conversations largely focused on tuition payments and his anxieties about his difficult work challenges.

So I decided to interview him about the book. I wanted to see what he thought, but also what he liked and what spoke to him. He said, "Let me tell you. I work in an environment that stresses diversity. Acceptance of multiculturalism and the need for tolerance. *Moby Dick* was ahead of its time."

He wears a green hoodie and a royal blue T-shirt. His glasses droop off of his nose and sit lopsided. He recently retired, but he taught at a school with a population of 80% Latino students. His first school in the Philadelphia School District had a 94% African American student body. Olney High School after that had the most even mix. It had Southeast Asians, blacks, Latinos, and whites.

Amber

This, for him was just like the Pequod. He thinks Melville particularly valued the racial harmony that he himself had experienced on whaling ships. In the novel we see several white characters, particularly Ahab, Ishmael, and the mates, but a number of major characters are non-white—Queequeg, Daggoo, Tashtego. Not to mention Pip and the cook. They got along very well because of their shared mission. He said, "They were all united to catch whales." Moreover, they coexisted because of Ahab's strong leadership.

As we're talking, Tashtego darts in and out of the bookshelves and Daggoo walks across the kitchen table. My Dad's cats continue this metaphor into his house. "I've become a cat-lover," he says. "I was all alone in the house. They're good companions." First he got Amber and Grise, which he pronounces as "*greeze*"–to stick to the French feminine for "gray." Together their names form "ambergris," the substance, which Stubb finds in the sperm whale's intestines. Melville writes, "Dropping his hands in he drew something that looked like ripe Windsor soap, or rich mottled cheese–very unctuous and savory withal. You might easily dent it with your thumb; it is of a hue between yellow and ash color."

Amber is orange and plods slowly through the room struggling under her weight, and Grise is spotted gray and tends to hide in the basement.

My father's third cat is Daggoo, named after the black sailor. He says, "I developed a wish to have a third cat so I went to the SPCA and I saw a black one and she struck me as being extraordinarily beautiful." He adopted her and named her "Daggoo," even though Daggoo, the crew member, is male. "I named the female Daggoo and I figured not a soul is going to know the original was male."

Daggoo was an "outdoor cat." She escaped from the house in the middle of the winter and stayed outside for eight whole days. He thought he'd never see her again. So a student gave him a calico cat with a black, red, and white coat. He named her "Tashtego" after the Native American crewmember of the Pequod. "I don't know whether this is Indian colors or not," he reflected matter-of-factly, "but it seems, maybe."

"Talk about creatures and their capacities," he says, "A cat *is* a predator. If two cats trap a mouse, you cannot save the mouse. The cats will rip that mouse to shreds." "They won't do that to a person but in relation to prey, Oh God," he sighed.

Race and color operate in the book on another level for him as well. The whiteness of the whale is very important to him as it is for

Ishmael. Ishmael says, "It was the whiteness of the whale above all things that appalled me." My Dad sees this as Melville's commentary on slavery and politics in the 19th century. The whale, for him, in its grotesqueness and abnormality, represented the political extreme of white supremacy. Melville's focus on the whale's color–the starkness of its color–suggests that "it is one thing to be white and another thing to be gung-ho white." The whiteness symbolized hatred, obsession, and injustice. "We're supposed to side with Ahab up to a point," he says, in his quest to eradicate the world of this evil. Ahab is also guilty of obsession, though, and this has political ramifications in my Dad's thinking as well. Ahab "represented for Melville the abolitionists who were too extreme." Though he made sure to point out that Melville might not have been thinking about Lincoln, he described the challenge of navigating between the political extremes of slaveholders and William-Lloyd-Garrison types. "If people had accepted more gradualism, maybe the civil war could have been avoided. Maybe not."

Daggoo

At one point in time, before his high school teaching career and before I was born, my Dad was a Judaic Studies scholar. He received an M.A. in Ancient and Jewish History from Columbia and earned a Ph.D. in Judaic Studies from Brandeis. He edited a collection about Jewish Women's Studies. He met my Mom, a rabbinical student, while teaching at Gratz Hebrew College in Philadelphia. From old faculty photos hung on the walls of that college I learned he had had a long brown beard and curly hair.

That was over 30 years ago. He still reads Torah occasionally at his local synagogue and he once talked of an intention to write an essay about Moses Mendelssohn, but I never knew him as a religious scholar. I only saw his deviations from traditional Jewish practice and dietary restrictions–the clam chowder in his freezer and Burger-King wrappers on the floor of his car. On our summer camping trips he would order for my brother, my sister, and me McDonald's "Happy Meals" without the hamburger–just the cheese, bun, french fries, and soda. He respected that we were kosher. At my Mom's house we had separate dishes for dairy and meat meals and we studied at a private Jewish Day School. In fourth grade I even wore *tzitzit,* the traditional fringed undergarment, at the behest of my Judaic Studies teacher.

The traces of his religious background still trickle through his reading of *Moby Dick*, though. He sees the book as an affirmation and commentary on biblical values, and symbols. Ahab and the whale "have to be symbols," he said, in the same definitive tone he used when playing the computer game Minesweepers, "This has to be a mine, that can't be a mine." For him, Ahab and the whale both are symbols of evil.

According to a traditional reading of the Bible whales are agents of God, particularly in the story of Jonah in which the leviathan answers Jonah's prayers and saves him from the tempestuous sea. In *Moby Dick* the opposite is true. The whales are malevolent creatures. Like earthquakes, hurricanes, and volcanoes they are, "incredible forces of nature that are not benign."

My Dad then paused, looked past me and nodded his head, "That was a *nasty* whale."

Grise

He said Melville's message is "that human beings must negotiate between two diametrically opposite forces." When I pushed him to define evil, he said, "Look. You take me and my development for example. I had to negotiate between my father and mother. Go pick. It wasn't easy. You know what I mean. Each one of them had negatives in his or her own way and it shifts and you don't know how to make *your* way. You have to constantly make decisions."

And then he retreated, "You're asking me to spell it out. Melville wouldn't ask us to spell it out. Ahab and the whale," he said, "are just two forces of evil."

And, finally, Ishmael. Ishmael, for him represented the objective middle ground between these two opposite forces. "He is a decent human being," my Dad stressed. "He is tolerant of Queequeg when others might not have been" and Melville makes a judgment, "Ishmael is the one person who clearly represents decency. He survives. This mirrors the biblical story of Jonah. 'Ishmael' in Hebrew means 'God hears,'" he told me. "And where Ahab is implacable, Jonah and the biblical Ishmael repent and God hears their prayers."

"Biblically, the character Ishmael also is an outsider. He is the son of Abraham and Hagar, and the matriarch Sarah expels him from the house. He is a reject. An exile."

In the Bible we learn of Ishmael's return to society, but in *Moby Dick* we predominantly see his retreat. "He didn't want to participate in society" and "he's open to the world, he wants to see the world, he doesn't want to be confined to the mainland. He wants to get out on the water, which is a wonderful point of view. I know people like that," my Dad says.

And yet, he, too, is an Ishmael. A self-styled outsider surrounding himself with a crew of cats trying to escape his parents and my mother. And just maybe he'll be able to see the world. On a drive down from Princeton he told me that in his retirement he wanted to make extra cash driving cars long distances for retirees. He said he liked seeing the scenery.

Prompt: In a dream the car salesman of the first car you ever owned told you to take the car for a three-hour spin. Write 300-500 words about that experience for posterity.

My New Car

My piece, since it relates a dream, thus reflects both feelings I have now in 2018 as well as feelings I had in 1967, 51 years ago. Predictably enough, the theme for me far transcends the car itself.

But first a word about *it.* It was a three-year-old eight-cylinder four-door 1964 Bel Air Chevrolet. I was told later that that model had the exact same engine as a Cadillac. My father noticed an advertisement of Clay Chevrolet Used Cars in Newton Corner, Massachusetts, in which the price of the car was $1100, an incredible bargain even for 1967 prices. When we inquired about the car at the dealer, the head salesman couldn't even find the vehicle, for it was a "loss leader" hidden in a corner, which the company might have preferred not to sell at all.

It was a phenomenal car. Though the prompt instructs me to write about my first three hours of owning it, I can't resist mentioning that from June to September of 1969 I took it on a 13,000-mile camping trip around the perimeter of the country–with extensive side trips in between. In those first three hours, however, I confess I had the mixed feelings that it was a big "unfashionable" American car. Spiffier foreign compact cars were coming into vogue; and I, in fact, was later to own a Toyota, a Subaru, and a Honda in turn. Perhaps an important reason I so love my 1994 GMC Jimmy now is that it is a sibling, or perhaps a scion, of my Chevrolet first love.

But, as I mentioned at the beginning of the piece, Clay Chevrolet was located in Newton Corner, Massachusetts; and therein lay a complication in my psyche. For I–having lived for the first 14 years of my life in the Roxbury section of Boston and the next seven in Brighton, leaving to study for a year in Jerusalem and two in Manhattan, before returning for six in Brighton again–had a "have-not psychology." I wonder whether many Bostonians do have one as well, severely aggravated by the "curse of the Bambino," alleged to have originated from the Red Sox's sale of Babe Ruth to the Yankees in December of 1919.

Do you know that the Town of Brookline is incorporated separately–though it is completely enclosed in the very heart of the City of Boston and is even in a different state county, Norfolk–from Boston, which is in Suffolk County? Also, that Norfolk County is a large one, extending all the way to Rhode Island in the south and that the part of Norfolk County that comprises Brookline is completely non-contiguous with the rest of that county. To be sure, the main reason for Brookline's anomalous geographical status has been the elitist wish of its residents not to be associated with less affluent Bostonians. Recognition of that fact used to make me feel ill at ease.

My unease extended to Newton, to the west of Boston and bordering the very western section of Boston, Brighton. Newton originally used to be considered "The Thirteen Villages of Newton," which are, in alphabetical order, Auburndale, Chestnut Hill, Newton Center, Newton Corner, Newton Highlands, Newton Lower Falls, Newton Upper Falls, Newtonville, Nonantum, Oak Hill, Thompsonville, Waban, and West Newton. A very close friend lived in Auburndale; my doctoral professor, whom I used to drive home from Brandeis in Waltham, lived in Newton Center; a first cousin lived in Waban; and my father and I, as I, of course, mentioned, bought my first car for me in Newton Corner.

Visiting any part of Newton and Brookline at any time–even for the exciting event of acquiring my first car–and dreaming about such until this day have given me the unwelcome anxiety of having grown up "on the wrong side of the tracks" that I have never fully outgrown.

Rabies Control in Philadelphia
by brother Rob

In my brother's *Genres Mélange Deuxième,* I recounted how my unexpected Philadelphia Department of Public Health (PDPH) career began. As it turned out, it was a journey which lasted 36 years and included a number of different administrative positions. During my last 14 years with PDPH I was the Director of the Division of Disease Control (DDC), the only non-physician to fill this position in PDPH's history. Briefly, the DDC is responsible for maintaining city-wide surveillance of over 55 diseases of public-health importance through mandated physician and laboratory reporting; identifying unusual occurrences of these diseases (outbreaks); and implementing steps to limit the further spread of these diseases. All of these diseases, of course, occur in humans, but one that we monitored–rabies–primarily occurs in four-legged animals, both wild and domesticated, and can spread from these animals to humans.

The PDPH began collecting and publishing data on disease occurrence in the early 1900s. From that time until the late 1980s/early 1990s, Philadelphia had no rabies in land animals (approximately 2% of bats may be rabid, totally unrelated to any rabies in land animals). This situation was destined to change, we learned, because raccoon hunters in North Carolina tired of hunting non-aggressive raccoons in their environs and brought in more aggressive ones from Florida, inadvertently importing some with rabies. From there over the next decade, rabies, primarily in raccoons, with some overflow into skunks and into the domestic cat and dog populations, inexorably spread throughout North Carolina, and into Virginia, Maryland, and Central Pennsylvania.

We knew it was only a matter of time until Philadelphia got its first case of rabies in an animal. We began alerting Philadelphia residents, and medical care providers, of the expected arrival of rabies in raccoons and advised them that pets must be vaccinated and not allowed to roam, especially at night. We partnered with local veterinarians, the SPCA, and the Philadelphia Fire Department; and we held a number of free rabies-vaccination clinics for pets in firehouses throughout the city.

With the Pennsylvania Game Commission, the PDPH developed a joint protocol for responding to Philadelphia residents reporting a "sick" raccoon or other animal on their property. This protocol called for a PDPH investigator to be the initial responder to assess the situation and, if deemed necessary, to then call the Game Commission to "put down" the possibly rabid animal. (Pennsylvania Game Commission members are the only enforcement individuals, other than members of the Philadelphia Police Department, who are authorized to fire their weapons within the city limits). The PDPH responder would then take possession of the dead animal and bring it to the PDPH laboratory for testing. After the appropriate preparation with laboratory reagents a piece of the dead animal's brain would be examined under a microscope. If positive for rabies, the specimen would fluoresce green. All positive specimens would also be sent to the Pennsylvania Department of Health for confirmation. In the event of a positive result, the PDPH would then re-contact the resident to ascertain whether there had been any human contact with the rabid animal. If there had been, the PDPH would then assess the nature of that contact and, if necessary, ensure that the person or persons involved receive a complete series of rabies immunizations.

Over the years I personally responded to many "sick animal" reports and got to know one Game Commission officer who responded to most requests for service. One particular report of a sick raccoon remains quite vivid in my memory.

One summer Sunday afternoon while on call I received a report from the City Hall operator of an alarmed woman reporting a sick raccoon on her property. When I learned of the caller's address, I realized that it wasn't far from my home and decided to respond myself, rather than contact the on-call investigator. I thus arrived at the woman's home in fewer than five minutes, which totally surprised her. Rather than being pleased at the rapidity of my response to her plea for help, however, she was initially quite suspicious of my presence, certainly because I had arrived so quickly, but also possibly because of my appearance. In my haste I hadn't changed out of my T-shirt, shorts, and sneakers. To allay the woman's suspicions, I showed her my credentials and asked to see the sick raccoon. Never leaving her porch, she pointed in the general direction where the raccoon had been, telling me that, when she had last seen it, it was on the other side of a chain-link fence which ran through her property. As I approached the fence, I saw the raccoon lying on its side gasping for breath, clearly in extreme distress. I then returned to the porch and called for the Game Commission officer to arrive.

I explained to the woman that we had to wait for the Game Commission officer, and she went back into her house, leaving me on the porch. After about five minutes she returned to the porch and asked whether she could ask me a question. Thinking that she was seeking more information about rabies, I said "Sure, what would you like to know?"

I was completely taken aback when she asked, "Do your parents know what you do for a living?"

Upon hearing that question, I thought to myself that my parents had absolutely no idea, and would be appalled to learn, that I went to people's houses to collect the dead bodies of potentially rabid animals. I could hear them lamenting that that was not what they had sent me to college and graduate school for. I laughed and told her that my parents had some general idea of my job, but didn't know the specifics, such as those that brought me to her doorstep. We laughed together and then waited for the Game Commission officer to arrive.

About 20 minutes later a jeep came screeching to a stop at the house and out jumped a man I had never seen before, dressed in, of all things, a tuxedo! Nor was he alone, for in the passenger seat of the jeep was a woman dressed in an ornate evening gown. Clearly my call had come at a most inopportune time for them; and, to say the least, neither one was at all pleased to have been summoned to this address. Without any introduction the man sharply asked where the raccoon was, and we pointed to the chain-link fence. The man then pulled a snub-nosed revolver from his cummerbund, moved quickly to the fence, and through an opening in the fence discharged his revolver twice. Without any further ado, he ran back to his jeep, jumped in, and the couple took off. When I went to pick up the body of the raccoon, I was shocked to see that it was still breathing. The Game Commission officer had totally missed his target–twice! I had no choice but to call for him to return. When he came back, he was more than a little agitated and without a word went back to where the raccoon was and this time stood over it and successfully put it out of its misery.

The story doesn't quite end there. The next day I received an excited call from the laboratory director. She had just completed the examination of the raccoon brain. She confirmed that the animal had been rabid–no surprise there–but added that the specimen fluoresced the brightest green of any of the hundreds of positive specimens that she had ever processed. She thanked me for collecting the specimen and told me that "it had made her day." To me, the laboratory result meant that the saliva of this raccoon, for whatever reason, contained more rabies virus than usual, and I reconfirmed with the woman on whose property the raccoon was found that there had been no human contact with it. I then returned to my other duties, thinking what strange things excite laboratory professionals–and how unexpected life occurrences can be.

I'm sure that all five of us who were involved in this episode have remembered it for a long time. I certainly have!

INTERPRETATION/REVIEWS

"Are You Being Served?"

My title is that of a popular British BBC sitcom which spanned 69 episodes from 1972 to 1985. PBS in South Florida now shows reruns on Saturday night, and Reva and I watch it faithfully. In fact, since I get my news and entertainment on AOL, the show is the only television that I *do* watch. *Wikipedia* is the source of much of my factual information in this piece–in its article on the show and in the several articles on the major actors. I begin by quoting: "Set in London, the show follows the misadventures and mishaps of the staff of the retail ladies' and gentlemen's clothing departments, in the flagship department store of a fictional chain called Grace Brothers." Even for a non-Anglophile, there is much to be enjoyed in the ironies and double-entendres of British humor and the quirks and foibles of the British personalities. Above all, the show spoofs the hierarchies of the British class system, still residually operative even among the staff of a clothing department in a large store. The show was created and written by Jeremy Lloyd and David Croft. Interestingly, Jeremy Lloyd has written that he had been sent at an early age to live with his grandmother and that he rarely saw his parents, who he claimed considered him a failure. His father withdrew him from prep school when he was 13, and he thereupon worked as a junior assistant in the menswear department at Simpson's of Piccadilly Circus. He drew many of the characters in the sitcom from his experiences there and from a job as a traveling paint salesman. He has stated his belief that his early jobs gave him a better education than a university could have provided.

The title of the show fascinates me, especially the interrogative verb in the passive voice, "Are You Being Served?"–the routine first question a British salesperson asks a customer. In America, I think, a customer must approach the salesperson for assistance, or, if the latter sees that she is needed, she will ask, "May I help you?" "Serving" clearly denotes the act of a subordinate in relation to a superior and reflects British hierarchical thinking–even in the area of sales. The passive voice softens the disparity of rank a little. In the active voice, "May I serve you?" is, well, too servile. I myself actually was jarred by the verb when I heard–in a visit to England in 1975–a woman asking a salesman forcefully, "Will you serve me?"

The main characters are:

- Mrs. Betty Slocombe. She is head of the ladies' department. She is known for her colorful hairdos and her conversations about her cat, which she always refers to as her "pussy."

- Miss Shirley Brahms. She is an attractive, working-class, Cockney-speaking, junior sales assistant to Mrs. Slocombe.

- Mr. Ernest Grainger. A 40-year veteran of Grace Brothers, he is head of the menswear department. He often falls asleep on the job and is usually grumpy.

- Mr. Wilberforce Claybourne Humphries. A sales assistant in menswear, he is described as "living with his mother." He acts and speaks in a gay manner and elicits tolerance in this respect from his co-workers.

- Mr. James "Dick" Lucas. A young, penniless, womanizing, junior salesman, he irritates the female staff.

- "Captain" Stephen Peacock. He is the "floorwalker," who directs customers to respective salespeople. He haughtily considers himself as ranking higher than the staff. He represents himself as having served in Africa in World War II, but he may have actually been in the Service Corp and may never have seen combat.

- Mr. Cuthbert Rumbold. He is the bumbling floor manager, autocratic to the staff, but obsequious to "Young" Mr. Grace, the department store owner.

- "Young" Mr. Grace. He is the very old, rich but stingy, owner, always surrounded by young women.

In polite society, one does not find names humorous, but some of them, just the same, such as Peacock, are meant to be satirical. Indeed, "Captain" Peacock does strut like a peacock. The dialogue, with rapid repartees, is non-stop funny. The situations, such as a temporary promotion of salesman Mr. Grainger to floor manager or the introduction of mannequins with moving parts, are uproarious. Reva and I recommend the show to you.

As Serious As He Is
Funny–Trevor Noah

Trevor Noah of Comedy Central has been described as "seriously funny"; but the truth is that, when he is funny, he is *very* funny and, when he is serious, he is very serious indeed. The fact of his being born "mixed race," and thus illegal, in the South Africa of *apartheid*– one of the main points of his autobiography *Born a Crime*[1]–is in no way funny.

Having a sense of humor, however, enables an individual to recognize the absurdities of the human condition and to transcend them. One such was when his ex-step-father Abel shot his mother Patricia through the back of the head and very nearly killed her. Her reports of domestic violence had been systematically ignored by the South African police for years and Abel's alcoholism and uncontrolled anger had been abnormal. His mother made a miraculous recovery and was out of the hospital in four days. In the hospital she had said to Trevor, "My child, you must look on the bright side." (page 281)

"Mom, you were shot in the face. There is no bright side."

"Of course there is. Now you're officially the best-looking person in the family."

One highly significant feature of Noah's life is his extraordinary facility in languages owing to his locations at the intersections of South African life. He speaks English, Xhosa, Zulu, Sotho, Tswana, Tsonga, Afrikaans, and German. He attributes to Nelson Mandela the insight that talking to a person in the person's language establishes heart-to-heart connections, for Mandela had said, "If you talk to a

---

[1] *Born a Crime: Stories from a South African Childhood.* New York: Spiegel & Grau, 2016.

man in a language he understands, that goes to his head. If you talk to him in his language, that goes to his heart." (page 236)

One of the most humorous accounts in the book is the story of his taking a beautiful young woman–Babiki–to his senior prom. But he got lost on the way, and they arrived two hours late. She was uncommunicative and refused to get out of the car. It turned out that one of the severe problems they had was that they did not speak the same language and, strangely enough, he hadn't been aware of that. She spoke only Pedi, a South African language he did not know.

After Noah had been hired in 2015 in his new position as replacement for Jon Stewart on Comedy Central, previous negative tweets of his against Jews and Israel–and more recently again tweets about Australian aboriginal women–"hit the fan." Two against Jews and Israel, respectively, were "Behind every successful Rap Billionaire is a double as rich Jewish rich man" (May 12, 2014) and "South Africans know how to recycle like Israel knows how to be peaceful." (June 2, 2010) Noah, however, has apologized for the indiscretions about Jews and Israel; and Rabbi Abraham H. Foxman, in a letter to *Time* entitled "Let's Not Prejudge Trevor Noah," wrote magnanimously, "I wish Mr. Noah great success as he moves into the anchor chair at Comedy Central. Despite his Twitter history, I'm ready to give him the benefit of the doubt. Let's not prejudge him based on a few, random, isolated tweets in the past. Let's judge him based on his performance going forward into the future."[2]

One funny–though perhaps not completely funny for Jews–story in *Born a Crime* was about Trevor's "DJ"ing a dance at a Jewish school and unintentionally scandalizing the administration by featuring a proficient dancer from the crew named "Hitler." For black South Africans, he explains, Cecil Rhodes ranks far higher on the scale of evil than Hitler; for the Congolese, the number-one evildoer was Belgium's King Leopold. The name "Hitler," on the other hand,

---

[2]   http://time.com/3765989/abe-foxman-lets-not-prejudge-trevor-noah/

simply symbolized a very tough white man. "This Hitler was so powerful that at some point black people had to go help white people fight against him–and if the white man has to stoop to ask the black man for help fighting someone, that someone must be the toughest guy of all time. So if you want your dog to be tough, you name your dog 'Hitler.' If you want your kid to be tough, you name your kid 'Hitler.' There's a good chance you've got an uncle named 'Hitler.' It's just a thing." (pages 194f.–[I have put the name in the quotation in single quotation marks.])

Born a Crime is chock-full of painful suffering, adolescent tribulations, hair-raising adventures, life on the margins, testing boundaries, trying to increase profits, warding off failure–but, above all, as Trevor's Mom put it, "looking on the bright side." And having a laugh whenever possible.

Devorah Baum's *Feeling JewISH* (a Book for Just About Anyone)

(New Haven and London: Yale University Press, 2017)

Devorah Baum has written an extraordinarily ambitious book centered on the theme of Jewishness as a metaphor for a person's complications, ambivalences, warring inner struggles, and multi-facetedness–but, above all, yearning for wholeness and peace of mind. She covers a wide range of topics in the disciplines of history, literature, and psychology and draws prodigiously on what seems an encyclopedic knowledge of sources. Virtually every paragraph of the book contains an insight or a new connection of ideas.

It is the treatment of emotions which is Baum's forte: such as self-hatred, envy, guilt, overcompensation, paranoia, mother love, and self-obsessiveness. Jews manifest all these emotions, Baum reasons; but others do as well and, to the extent that they do, they don't recognize just how "Jew*ish*" (note the italicized "*ish*" suffix) they are. There is no way a single reviewer can plumb the depths of the book. I daresay specialists in history, literature, and psychology, respectively, can profitably write several essays each on the multiplicity of topics covered in each area.

Baum's main emphasis is that sharing among individuals resolves interpersonal contradictions and that this sharing helps clarify inner conflicts within individuals as well. I find it most interesting that the author's "Acknowledgments" section comes at the very end of the book and that in its last paragraph she mentions her conflict in accepting her husband's constructive criticisms, but, above all, values the "lovely shared world" of her family. (274)

It is the contradictions, nay contradictoriness, that Baum bridges which strike me very forcefully. Of the hundreds of examples of these/this in the book, let me quote just one—about paranoia: "To view paranoid delusions through the lens of a simple binary of true/false, right/wrong, fails to comprehend the reason within the madness in a manner that ironically also mirrors in its binary thinking the madness within our reason." (169)

There are two major omissions in the book, which I infer are both analogous and purposeful; and they are feelings of both Jews (and non-Jews) about the question of the importance of adherence to religious traditions, on the one hand, and about the State of Israel, on the other. Just as the author in one aside mentions that she keeps kosher, (39) she makes another brief comment about Israel's oppression of Palestinians. (184) Her attitude to her own traditional religiosity and her attitude to the modern Israeli Jew's valuation of the assertion of power must certainly be too important in her consciousness to be ignored in an otherwise comprehensive study of Jewish emotions and their significance, both universal and particularized.

"*Gornisht Helfen*" (It's No Use)

The central word play of this piece is that the Yiddish phrase "*gornisht helfen*"–which means "nothing helps" or "it's no use"–and is the first half of the book-review mill's "Gornisht Helfen. Laughables" company name as referred to derisively by writers in the know also applies to useless and unusable reviews of said company. Did I write "said company"? I could have warmed to "sad company" as well, except that President Trump's overuse of "sad" in his tweets irritates me.

As a satirist, I believe I am within my rights to lampoon a company's disinterest in truth for ignoble purposes, especially since I paid the company hundreds of dollars for a contemptible review of a book of mine. My title and my first paragraph are satirical. I now begin a straightforward essay.

I surmise that one purpose of the company is projecting a style of "jaded chic." I have been developing in my writing an understanding of a multiplicity of personae that I go by and of the tailoring of my different personae to individuals in different relationships. For example, my son Judah calls me "DAP" (for "Dad/*Abba*/*Pater*"), but my daughter Aliza and son Benjy simply call me "*Abba.*" The reviewer, with little psychological depth, described my interest in personae as "navel-gazing."

Let me unburden myself of the fear that the company, threatened by being exposed for what it is, will sue me for quoting, however minimally, from its review–even though I have expressly forbidden that the review be published. Neither have I mentioned here the real name of the company, nor given the name of my book. I am assured by Xlibris book consultants that Xlibris has expert intellectual-property lawyers who vet my writings, including this piece, for anything not passing legal muster.

My Xlibris books have been multi-genres collections. I understand from my creative-writing teacher Chris Notarnicola of Florida Atlantic University that such collections might be becoming more standard. "Humor" is as important to me as any other genre or category. (The category of "Word Play" has not been established as a genre; perhaps that may yet come to be.)

At any rate, the reviewer unabashedly stated that "Memoirs" is "the book's strongest section."

I have no argument that it is strong, but why the invidious disparagement of the other four sections? I fault the reviewer for being "insensitive to the author's purposes."

I raised numerous objections to the review with the company's editorial office, one of which was "open-and-shut." The reviewer insisted in designating my Hebrew Scripture interpretations as "Old Testament" ones, though I never once in my book had used the latter term.

One ludicrous justification of arbitrary, subjective, unsubstantiated criticism was "opinion-based analysis"–as in the case of a comment that the book is "an odd collection of thoughts and stories that never quite gel." I am reminded of a high-school student who defended a false assertion with the statement that he had a right to his opinion. I had a thought in relation to the reviewer that if he or she had read the book with the care it deserved its organization would have made better sense.

"Opinion-based analysis"–What a lark! What a fallacious contradiction in terms!

I am embarrassed for the company!

A summation from no less than Shakespeare himself comes to mind: "Something is rotten in the state of Denmark!"

In the Time of the Butterflies
CLOSE READING

by daughter Aliza Levenson,
for her course with Professor Karen Bishop,
"Human Rights in Latin American Literature,"
February 10, 2011

"'You and Trujillo,' Papa says a little loudly, and in this clear peaceful night they all fall silent. Suddenly, the dark fills with spies who are paid to hear things and report them down at Security. *Don Enrique claims Trujillo needs help running this country. Don Enrique's daughter says it's about time women took over the government.* Words repeated, distorted, words recreated by those who might bear them a grudge, words stitched to words until they are the winding sheet the family will be buried in when their bodies are dumped in a ditch, their tongues cut off for speaking too much."

Julia Alvarez starts off the second-to-last paragraph on page 10 of *In the Time of the Butterflies* with the accusation, "You and Trujillo." In starting off this passage with "you," Alvarez automatically sets up an oppositional relationship with its referent "Trujillo." This oppositional relationship of "you," Minerva Mirabel, "and Trujillo," marries Minerva and Trujillo into an inextricable relationship–a relationship that will always be in opposition and a relationship that is bound until either the "you" or the "Trujillo" ceases to exist. In beginning this section with an opposition–with a conflicting and impossibly escapable relationship of two, Alvarez starts off the passage with hostility. The "you" followed by "and Trujillo" further complicates the relationship because the "you" precedes Trujillo, placing Minerva as the one who allows this opposition–as the one who commands the relationship....

In beginning the passage with "You and Trujillo," Alvarez automatically indicates that these two beings, Minerva and Trujillo, are enemies and will always stay enemies.... Their relationship is time-sensitive and also space-sensitive because both Minerva and Trujillo singularly occupy space in time as well as occupy spatial area. This occupation of both space and time shows how their relationship inhabits multiple oppositions, where space and time work as a framing binary for Minerva and Trujillo. These first three words of the passage, but specifically the "you" and the "Trujillo," provide a double lens through which it is possible to understand the passage–the passage functions through relations and in opposition to this first clause.

Alvarez describes Papa's remark as one that is said "a little loudly," where these words stand in contrast with each other. "Little" is a word that denotes an amount that is especially small; it is used to emphasize that Papa's remark has the possibility to be louder, but instead his words come out meekly. "Little" is "often coupled with some other adjective implying smallness[1]; here it is tied to "loudly" in a relationship of coexistence. Something that is said "loudly" is something that is said powerfully, vehemently, and with noise; however, in this instance, the way Papa delivers his comment it is not allowed to be powerful. His intonation must contrast with the inherently aggressive words that come out of his mouth because this first clause frames the rest of the passage. "Little" contrasts with "loudly," but they necessitate each other because when combined in a contrasting relationship where "little" plays an important role in softening the coming noise, they work to massage the hostility of the first clause. Both descriptors are strikingly different where "little" designates a small, less important thing and "loudly" stands for something that is inherently important. The juxtaposition of these two words allows for Papa's comment to work in multiple ways– his intonation contrasts in and of itself, his actual words stand in opposition, and his intonation stands in opposition to the words. Throughout the passage Alvarez heavily uses the literary device of consonance, wherein consonance appears with different letters that have alternate effects. In the first sentence alone, there is a

---

[1]   http://www.oed.com.proxy.libraries.rutgers.edu/

series of connected "l" sounds that roll off the tongue and have the onomatopoeic effect of lulling. In this first sentence there are nine instances of this lulling with the "l", where in two of these instances, the "l" s appear consecutively–"... little loudly and in this clear and peaceful night they all fall silent." This set of "l" s gives the sentence a calming effect. The placement of the "l" envelops the sentence–the "l" sound starts off as appearing twice in the first two words of the pattern and then there is a lesser amount in the middle of the sentence followed with a torrent of "l" s in the last three words. This dissonant placement of "l" s is strategic because it allows the sentence to work reflexively. It works reflexively because the first and last "l"s both appear in clauses that refer to sound; the "l"s in the first and last words are self-referential. The first instance, as mentioned above, is a weakened exclamation of one that should be louder, whereas the last words with "l" s all refer to the complete opposite of something *loud*–*silence*. The **"l"** s of **"little loudly"** oppose **"all fall** silent" because of the nature of the message–that Papa speaks somewhat "loudly" but then everyone becomes "silent," where these words oppose each other as well as counteract the hostility of the beginning accusation.

This lulling effect is contrasted with the callous sounds of the "t" in the very last sentence of the passage. Their difficult reality is presented in this last sentence and the "t" sound allows this harsh reality to emanate from the words. After beginning the passage employing the use of soothing consonants, Alvarez ends this passage with "**t**ongues cu**t** off for speaking **t**oo much." This phrase does not act self-oppositionally, but instead, it acts in relation to the first sentence as a response. The biting "t" sound is necessary in this sentence. It implicitly references torture with tongue removal, because it opposes the softness of the first sentence and works with the bite of the first clause.

These fragments from the first and last sentence of the paragraph are bound together in a relationship that frames the passage as one that is both peaceful and torturous, where silence is emblematic of peace as well as symbolizes a break in the relationship of "You and Trujillo."

Paper Podium: the Voice of Affinity

"Paper Podium: the Voice of Affinity" is a slender 95-page volume of 91 poems, composed by a remarkable thoughtful and sensitive voice indeed, that of Joseph E. Bruno–known to us in the Kings Point Creative Writers Club as "Joe." He is the epitome of *"simpatico,"* for which I will give a fitting English equivalent here, "affinitive." A short review can hardly do justice to the range, wisdom, power, and beauty of the collection. My brief treatment of a number of selected poems exemplifying different aspects of the poet's creativity can only give the reader hints of what the book contains.

METER AND RHYME–The poet likes iambic and anapestic in tetrameter. "Offspring" (page 7) is in the former, and "Dreaming Together" (page 14) is in the latter. The poems are in rhyming couplets.

"With words and paint and clay I give,
A part of me I hope will live.
An object fashioned with a bond.
Heart to hands to soul respond."

"I've got a heart full of wonder every day,
Since we both started dreaming together this way.
Across so many miles, we share something new,
When you're dreaming of me, I'm dreaming of you."

METAPHOR, METER, and ALLITERATION–The poem "Writers' Blocks" (page 23) contains the exquisite double meaning of "block." Joe describes the challenge of writing in terms of constructing a building with stone blocks. This poem is in trochaic tetrameter.

"Cornerstone, first to be set.
Characters that must be met.
Ponder, question, try in place.
Squaring edges, smoothing face.

No easier to choose the next.
Building rows of blocks into text.
Another row falls up with ease.
Then impasse, none hewn to please.

Anxiety at every try.
Leading questions into my
Ever deeper quarry pit
To find the block that will be fit.

The rush of time, I was unknowing.
My focus on the stone wall growing.
One more piece, the work is capped.
Elastic stretch of time is snapped."

The poem contains the alliterative pattern of a thread of "c's, "ck's, "q's, and hard "g's, It reinforces the theme of energy, purpose, and resolving difficulty. There is onomatopoeia, furthermore, in the soft "ch" and "sh" digraphs. The "sh" of "rush" in "rush of time" evokes the interjection "Whoosh." "That word rush"; "choose," in "to choose the next"; and "stretch," in "elastic stretch of time," represent a second alliterative pattern, which contrasts with the first one. It signifies the transcendent creative process, the vitality of the poet's mind, the fluidity of his thought, and the confidence that problems get solved and anxiety dissipates with determination and the passage of time. One could spend a whole class on this one poem alone. Just two last items, as a case in point. "Falls up" in "Another row falls up with ease" is a brilliant irony. It comprises four different meanings in one. In the case of the laying of stone blocks, the rows mount higher and higher. But, if an earthquake should strike, the rows might "fall down" or "fall in." Yet in the case of writing a poem, the words and the rows "fall in place."

The word "elastic" is mimetic. Its etymology is the Greek "stretched out." The word itself stretches out, but its final "c" represents that the stretching does have a limit, reaching which it "snaps." The "snapping" is artfully ambiguous. Does the poet mean "breaking" or "resuming the original shape"? Perhaps he means both. Perhaps, interactively, he wants to leave that question up to the reader.

IRONIC ENDINGS–Joe's wisdom is evident in the power of his frequent ironic closing couplets. A few examples have to suffice.

In "Full-Moon Circle" (page 45), "Some life circles can't be seen 'til we look back to where we've been."

In "The Healer" (page 51), "By practice, this healer does find, Most healing lives within the mind."

In "The Fool" (page 59), "His blessing on the feasting hall, Some ask if he's a fool at all."

In "Softly Guided" (page 71), "Farther ahead than we can see, We are the path of what can be."

LOVE OF NATURE–The Table of Contents announces a rich feast from "The Bat" (page 4) to "Maples' Time" (page 20) to "Daisytime" (page 26) to "Bear Tree" (page 36) to "Spring Pond" (page 50) to "Slant Rock" (page 91).

SPIRITUAL MYSTERIES–Legends "speak respect to elders' spirit" in "Tribe" (page 22). Artifacts tell stories and "enlightened seers" interpret icons in "Totems, Lost and Found" (page 29). Mythology about the planets and constellations is the content of "Skylights" (page 31).
The poet invokes the Spirits (with a capital "S") of the Bear, Hawk, Wolf, Sun, and Earth" in "A Calling" (page 42). He calls a sixth Spirit "Great Turtle," in "Good Spirits' Call" (page 52), suggesting with confidence that they will respond.

The 91 poems, in sum, are both enlightening and exhilarating.

Swear More

I am happy to review Emma Byrne's new book *Swear!ng Is G*od f*r You: The Amaz!ng Sc!ence of Bad Language.* Interestingly, the author incorporates in her title two literary features–word painting and irony–gifted writers exemplify. For example, she intends her exclamation points substituting for "i" and "o" vowels to represent swear words in conversation.

The word "science" in the subtitle is important because Byrne bases her conclusions on scientific research. Accordingly, swearing derives from the processing of the right brain, where emotions are converted into speech. Though right-brain-injured people in the 1800s reduced to what seemed to be mere inchoate swearing alone used to be considered to have become nothing more than savages, neurobehaviorists now know that swearing communicates various kinds of deep emotion–response to pain, humor, and bonding with the group–not just simple aggression.

I, as a writer, seek more freedom to use mild profanity in my pieces because I feel it can expand my "expressive range." Here's an example. I wrote about a quip I made once to a student who expressed perplexity about what to call me, "Mr. Levenson" or "Dr. Levenson." "That doesn't matter to me. Just don't call me, 'Asshole!'"

Considering my epithet afterwards as an effective rapport-building comment, I quoted it to a colleague. Unexpectedly, she was critical of me. "A teacher's profanity of any sort, however mild, in class is demeaning. You needed to be a proper role model, but instead you lowered yourself to the students' level."

Recently, to make an impression in a Facebook comment, I used the "F-word." My friend Jack Cohen commented in turn in Yiddish (and in a Yiddish font to boot), "Eddie, what is this '*modernishe sprache*'?" Byrne, I am convinced, on the other hand, would have supported me heartily in both cases.

Swearing correlates with aggressiveness and reduces two kinds of pain: physical and social. But there is a differential effect for men and women. Societally, women are expected to be "nicer" than men. That extends to expectations that they not swear, and that affects that they utilize swearing less than men as a relief from pain.

Tourette's Syndrome involves involuntary ticcing and is often accompanied by involuntary anti-social swearing. It causes the sufferer very great distress; but researchers have discovered, nonetheless, that the higher quantity of dopamine released into the brain at the peak of the symptomatology indicates a certain pleasure as well.

As a woman needing to be accepted as an equal in a male-dominated field, Byrne states that swearing facilitates bonding. "Calling some equipment a fucking piece of shit is often a necessary rite of passage when I join a new team." (page 2)

The preceding exclamation works because it is not directed at an individual and is thus not threatening. "Jocular abuse," likewise, works when it stays "within the boundaries that people set for themselves...[or is] so outrageous that it can't possibly be meant seriously." (pages 97f.)

In a section called "Swearing as Rhetoric," Byrne illustrates that one's interpolations of "damn it" reinforce one's conviction and credibility. It's a matter of "getting your damn point across." (page 111)

She brings evidence from the animal kingdom that chimpanzees learn how to swear, such as with their signing for "Dirty" by bringing the back of the wrist against the underside of the chin. It's analogous to the human middle-finger gesture.

One authoritative study has established that multi-lingual people tend to swear mostly in their first language because that's the language in which they feel "most emotionally competent." (page 184) Byrne adds that swear words cannot be translated indiscriminately into other languages because of differential taboos and ranges of meaning. The evolutionary psychology of the human species has depended on the effective communication of individuals and groups for fight or flight. Byrne concludes her book (page 200) with the summation that swearing is essential in our continuing development to help us bear pain, work together, and express emotions.

WEIRD in a World That's Not

Jennifer Romolini's *WEIRD in a World That's Not: A Career Guide for Misfits, F*ckups, and Failures* is the most significant guide in applied psychology, human relationships, and positive thinking that I have read in a long time. The book is not my first experience of a benevolent usage of "weird." My daughter Aliza has described me as such, clarifying that it means that I am not boring. Aliza's description, in fact, has decisively influenced my interest in the word; and that is what led me to Romolini's book.

Shakespeare–more negatively–in calling the three witches in *Macbeth* "the weird sisters," suggests that they grasp the workings of human fate, "*wyrd*" meaning "fate" in Old English. Romolini, on the other hand, instructs readers how to aspire to fortunate destinies.

I restrict myself here to a focus on the author's different types of humor, so important as they are in extending warmth and establishing trust. I hope to review the themes of the book more comprehensively in another place.

The author's expressive profanity is a continuous *tour de force*. For one whose nervous tension rises from fingertips to elbows, "not giving an actual fuck" and like phrases release anxiety in the opposite direction right out of my body. A vulgarity-specializing comic once illustrated use of the "f-word" in all seven parts of speech. I don't remember how it served as a conjunction. *WWTN:CGMF*F* might be enlisted as an indispensable profanity anthology and reference work for this and other questions.

The book's use of upper-case words for emphasis is quite creative: "Don't leave notes. Notes are never a good idea. Notes make people unhappy, and they make them shame-spiral, and then you have people whose shame leads them to anger and spite, and then ANYTHING

CAN HAPPEN. Including a NOTE that answers YOUR NOTE. It's a NOTE OFF! Nobody wants this."

The innovative "shame-spiral" and the allusive "NOTE OFF" are noteworthy–but, Heaven forbid, not to be noted on a post-it.

Romolini describes office bosses, one of them representing "three modes: nervous, spazzing, yelling." In an example of the creative footnotes throughout the book, she adds in connection to this boss:

"Throughout my career, I've witnessed this pathology: some people, as soon as they gain even a glimmer of power, become dismissive and cruel to underlings, as if the office were a space where they felt free to let their inner creep loose–screaming, demanding, crying, behaving in ways that are childish and unreasonable because they know their assistants have no recourse but to endure the abuse. These same people can be warm and gregarious in the rest of their lives, and charm the business slacks off anyone they deem 'important.' A true mark of a person's goodness and integrity is how she treats her assistants–and waiters. End rant."

The phrases "inner creep" and "charm the business slacks off" deftly convey the author's understanding of sexual harassment in the office; and her concluding "End rant" minimizes the social distance among herself, peers, subordinates, and readers. Her emphasizing "a true mark of a person's goodness and integrity" highlights indirectly how very much she herself embodies those sterling qualities. For my purpose in the review, I have wanted to call to the reader's attention the humorous thoughts amidst the serious ones; but the serious ones are, of course, not to be underestimated.

In Romolini's career, her influence in the workplace increased, power shifted, she became a "boss" herself, and she understood "weirdness" in subordinates. She writes that she had difficulty getting raises for subordinates "because the person handling finances was a disorganized mess with her head up her ass" and that one employee–who did not keep "shit in perspective"–asked her about a raise "EVERY SINGLE DAY." "Weirdness," in the case of the two employees described in the quotation–the disorganized one and the nag–is *my* designation here, not the author's. In the context of the book, the advice is that self-defeating, anxiety-provoking, uncommonsensical behavior can be corrected so that people will be better integrated in the workplace with each other.

To be sure, I consider the book's focus on "weird" to be disingenuous–a strategy of humorous self-deprecation in analyzing individuals' lack of confidence and giving power over themselves to others. Discussing humor specifically here in the first section of my book [*GM*], I cannot praise *WWTN:CGMF*F* enough for its great appeal in attracting readers to delve deeply into the basics of human interrelationship.

MÉLANGE

Pro Xlibris Meque!
(To Xlibris and Me!)

Mi nove liber generum primus "Mélange"[1]
Inter alios meos haud sui generis[2]
De Xlibris[3] gloriam ad maximam suam
Bonum mundi summumque et felicis auctoris.

My first "Mélange"-named genres mix is here, Among my other books not that unique, Cheers, Xlibris, for your greater glory
And the greatest good of all and happy author.

My gratitude to Xlibris unbounded
For will to write and pride in its production
Unusual a tribute to one's self-publisher,[4]
But heartfelt all the more to one and all.

"Asot sfarim harbeh eyn qets"[5]—*LO "sof davar."*[6]
Tomorrow and tomorrow and tomorrow, God be willing.
More books! To life! *L'hayyim!*[7] It's very thrilling![8]

---

[1]   This ode was written on the occasion of the publication of my *Genres Mélange* (October 2017).

[2]   It is not "sui generis," because both *"Edward's Humor" and More* (February 2017) and *Genres Mélange Deuxième* (July 2018) are also multi-genres collections.

[3]   www.Xlibris.com.

[4]   This very sonnet, and see my "Introduction and Acknowledgments" section, page 9, in *Genres Mélange*.

[5]   "Of making many books there is no end."–It is ironic that both the Hebrew and the English are in the iambic rhythm.

[6]   "*Sof davar*" (the end of the matter)–Ecclesiastes 12:13. In Ecclesiastes a pious ending follows: "Fear God and observe His commandments." I have added the Hebrew word "LO" (not), turning verses 12 and 13 on their head: "It is not the end of the matter to say that there is no end of books. We want more Xlibris books."

[7]   Hebrew for "To Life!"

[8]   I have added a third line to the volta (the turn), making a 15-line sonnet and lines 14 and 15 a rhyming couplet.

145

Thea Aeide (As Known Down Here)

Aeide, Thea (as addressed in the Other Dimension)

Aeide Thea introduced herself to me—at a moment of great need during the Coronavirus inactivity—as the 20th contributor to our anthology. I wanted very much to round out the number of contributors to 20, a solid number with heft. The number 19 had symbolized for me the pain of the 19th prayer added centuries ago to the weekday *"Amidah"* (Standing) prayer of the Jewish liturgy, which beseeches the Almighty to foil slanderers and to destroy evil. She is a Transcendent Reality for me—though in a Jabèsian (I'll be explaining that approach elsewhere, to be sure) non-supernatural sense; but she also reveals herself in human form as Thea Aeide. I am moved by the "coolness" of her first name, Thea. I do represent her transcendent self in the cloud on the top right of the cover—*"thea,"* after all, means "goddess" in Greek. Readers may recall that the small-globe prototype on the cover of the 2018 anthology had been the domain of deceased member I. Irving Rosenberg. In this context I pay respects to deceased member Karen Gula as well.

"Aeide" and *"thea"* are the second and third words of the first line of Homer's *Iliad*; and resonating very deeply to it, I thrilled also in analogous admiration of the first lines of Vergil's *Aeneid* and of Genesis in Hebrew Scriptures—and then composed as an introduction to the anthology my own line, which alludes to ideas and features of the other three. The line of the *Iliad* does not precede the line of Genesis in historical meaning, but I list it first because the word *"aeide"* (sing), beginning as it does with an *"alpha"* (A), serves my symbolization of Aeide Thea/Thea Aeide as the first contributor to the collection in alphabetical order, based on the Greek original in which the word *"aeide"* precedes *"thea."* (Even if the other contributors would be alphabetized according to their first names, she would still precede Anne Rockwerk.) So the *"aeide"* line is the first of the four, just as Aeide Thea/Thea Aeide is the first of the 20 contributors.

Here are the four inter-allusive lines in Greek, Latin, Hebrew, and Latin, respectively. The first, second, and fourth are in a dactylic (long-short-short vowels) rhythm. Don't push that too far for the third; Hebrew metrics are different.

1. *"Menin aeide thea Peleiadeo Achilleos"*
   (Sing, O Goddess, of the resentment of Achilles, son of Peleus), *Iliad*
2. *"Arma virumque cano Troiae qui primus ab oris"* [*venit*]
   (I sing of arms and a man who first [came] from the shores of Troy), *Aeneid*
3. *"B'reshit bara Elohim et hashamayim v'et ha'arets"*
   (At the beginning of God's creating the heavens and the earth), Genesis
4. *"Anthologiam cano secundam familiae nostrae"*
   (I sing of the second anthology of our family), Yours Truly of the Kings Point Creative Writers Club and the Kings Point Writers Club Supplementary

Now for explication. The Goddess invoked by Homer is Calliope, the Muse of epic poetry. Homer's imperative verb for "sing" is the Greek *"aeide."* *"Cano"* in the Latin versions is a clear allusion to the former. Two (equally far-out) interactive anachronistic interpretations of *"aeide"/"cano"* are that they are prophetic anticipations of Yours Truly's wife's mother Ada, on the one hand, and the Major League Baseball star Robinson Canó, of New York Yankees, Seattle Mariners, and New York Mets fame.

The four lines taken together involve composite thematic unity. The strife in the *Iliad* dissipates when Achilles finally receives the respect he deserves. The hero Aeneas in the *Aeneid* exemplifies how great a difference a determined individual can make. God's creative power, wisdom, and love in Scripture are replicated in the endeavors of writers, singly and in groups.

A homiletical postscript. The first letter of *"aeide"*–"A"–leads us to appreciate all the other letters of the alphabet as well. The Hebrew letter "*bet*," and the Latin letter "C"–which, on their sides, look like cups facing inward in the respective directions of leftward in Hebrew and rightward in Latin–encourage readers to delve into the material, not looking up, down, or backwards. Indeed, that is why, as it is said, the first letter of Genesis begins with a "*bet*," not an "*aleph*." That having been said, readers, enjoy our second anthology starting anywhere you please.

I almost forgot. As my special Muse of this anthology–wife Reva is my overall Muse–Aeide Thea/Thea Aeide has inspired me to republish my Latin ode to my publisher Xlibris, which appeared on page vii in my *Genres Mélanges Deuxième* (July, 2018). It immediately preceded this invocation in this book.

These Are a Few of
My Favorite Things

Edmond Jabès
Great Inspiration
Particles
Wordplay
Edward R's Personae
Have their say
"Occude" and "Qvell"
How very apt
Check Wordnik out
And you'll be rapt
Reva my Diva
Love of my life
Quippes
Be you sure of that
Scrabble
Win-to-lose ratio's flat
Quite pious wife
With heart of gold
Enduring joy
We'll never grow old
Rob my brother
And Loudell
Gifts from Heaven
I don't tire to tell
Children give *nachas*[1] much
A cornucopia I'm not going to touch
Cousins getting along
As it is such
Natalie, Barbara,

---

[1]   Yiddish. A parent's emotional satisfaction and pride

And Judy, too
Judys do number three
Judy W., Judy B., and Judi Z.[2]
Colleagues in Writers Club
Wondrous exemplars
At 1 p.m. on Wednesdays a happy hub
Almost all of the time
"Good People"
Testifying I'm
Exciting production
Excellence of expression
No need for reduction
Proud editor
Accomplishment significant
Fulfillment extraordinary
No problem with creditor
Aggravations some
Irritating messings
They pale in comparison
To the overwhelming blessings

---

[2] Of Blessed Memory, Deceased on June 26, 2020

Introducing Édouard Zola ben Zola: His "I Affirm!"

First, a *bissel* (a little) biography. As I just hinted–and did not intend as a tribal wink, loving all as I do, just wanting to create an alliterative thread–I *am* Jewish. Émile Zola was my great French forbear, but I am not his biological descendant. I have taken his last name and added a metaphorical patronymic to convey my spiritual indebtedness to one of the world's greatest fighters for freedom, honesty, and truth in all of human history. Readers need no introduction to him.

I must state at the outset that I am not "cheap" or "stingy." The name "Zola" did not derive from the Hebrew "*zol*." Nor am I a glutton–Hebrew "*zolel*"–through I have been finding it hard to diet.

Enough preliminaries, and no more humor. I just needed to get your attention for the serious things I feel impelled, nay driven, to say. Please sit down firmly in your seats.

I AFFIRM that everyone everywhere should respect the legacy of Émile Zola.

I AFFIRM that self-interest can stifle "the better angels of our nature" (Abraham Lincoln).

I AFFIRM that democracy is the best form of government and of social organization.

I AFFIRM that citizens of countries, cities, towns, and villages–and members of associations–need to maintain vigilance against the subversion of noble values for elitist, antidemocratic purposes.

I AFFIRM that one must oppose close-minded selfishness and the power-seeking of the few.

I AFFIRM my belief that readers young and not-so-young, near and far, female and male, athletic and less-so identify with my affirmations.

Bonjours! Á Toujours!

Edward R. Levenson
May 14, 2020

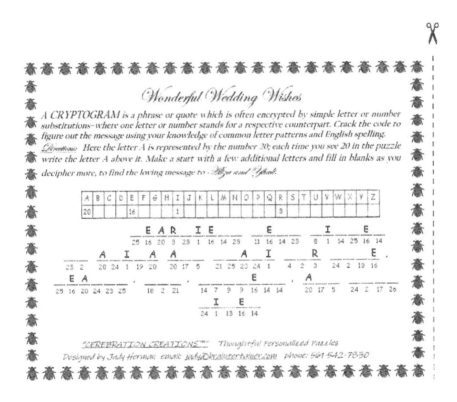

Wonderful Wedding Wishes

A CRYPTOGRAM is a phrase or quote which is often encrypted by simple letter or number substitutions–where one letter or number stands for a respective counterpart. Crack the code to figure out the message using your knowledge of common letter patterns and English spelling.

Directions: Here the letter A is represented by the number 20; each time you see 20 in the puzzle write the letter A above it. Make a start with a few additional letters and fill in blanks as you decipher more, to find the loving message to *Aliza and Yitzak*.

A	B	C	D	E	F	G	H	I	J	K	L	M	N	O	P	Q	R	S	T	U	V	W	X	Y	Z
20				16				1																	3

```
    E   A     I  E            E          I     E
   25  16 20  9 23  1  16 14 23    11 16 14 23   8  1  14 25 16 14

      A     I     A     A            A     I        R          E   ,
   23  2   20 24  1  19 20    20 17  5   21 25 20 24  1    4  2  3    24  2 19 16

   E  A              ,           ,          E        ,    A
  25 16 20 24 23 25     18  2 21    14  7  9  9 16 14 14    20 17  5   24  2  17 26

                    I     E
                  24  1  13 16 14
```

CELEBRATION CREATIONS™ Thoughtful Personalized Puzzles

Designed by Judy Herman; email: judy@celebertainer.com phone: 561-542-7830

152

HEARTIEST BEST WISHES TO
ALIZA AND YHALI
FOR LOVE, HEALTH, JOY, SUCCESS,
AND LONG LIVES

The Pawn Shop
by wife Reva

Her name was Rho and her father, who was a chemist, named her after the element Rhodium which has the atomic number of 45. In fact Rho's father was both pleased and amazed that at the age of 45 he had his first and only child. Rho romanticized her name as signifying the atomic number and as being associated with the Greek word "*rhodon*," which means "rose." Her mother was an inventor in the line of improving military weapons.

Rho's brilliant parents taught their precious daughter to be kind and thoughtful to all people. When her mother gave her a doll, she taught the little girl to say, "Thank you." When she asked her father for a ball, he said, "Say 'please' when you ask for something."

When Rho had been playing outside at age four, she came home sobbing and showed her mother bite marks on her hand from a girl next door. Her upset mother approached the child's mother and related the incident. The mother of the three-year-old girl said with remorse, "My daughter has a terrible habit of biting children. I'll hold her and, Rho, you bite her back."

"I can't hurt a girl who is smaller than me."

Rho's parents were proud of their child's kindness. The only disappointment they experienced was that their beautifully behaved daughter hadn't inherited their genius genes since she had only average intelligence. The report cards she gave them to sign had all "A's in Deportment, but only passing grades in academic subjects. She was outstanding, however, in Phys Ed; and they provided her with ice-skating lessons in the winter and dancing lessons the rest of the year.

After Rho graduated from business school, she went to work as a typist in a law office in Manhattan. She had high cheekbones, a big heart, and a striking appearance; and Madison Strauss, one of the legal clerks where Rho worked, became entranced with her. He rubbed the back of his neck and shifted his feet when he first approached her. "Would you like to have a coffee in Joe's Italian restaurant around the corner after work?"

Rho, in a light tone of voice, said, "Why yes, thank you."

They sat opposite each other at a table with a checked red and white tablecloth and Madison nervously nibbled on the knuckle of his left hand. Rho's stomach growled with hunger. Madison asked in halting stilted speech if Rho would like something to eat. She hesitated since she knew Madison was not earning much and had heard that he was supporting his sick mother. "No thank you," she said. "My mother has prepared dinner at home."

Madison subsequently made it a habit for both of them to drop into the restaurant for coffee after work. It took a few weeks before he got the nerve to ask her to go to the zoo on Sunday. They dated steadily for a year–strolling in the park, sitting on the boardwalk at Coney Island, and roller skating. One evening under the stars on a bench in Central Park, Madison said in a quivering voice, "I love you, Rho. Will you marry me?"

"I don't know," Rho said, as she clenched her fists. "You'll have to ask my father."

With a high-pitched quick laugh Madison said, "But I don't want to marry your father. I want to marry you!"

Rho's father met Madison and approved of him. After he gave his permission, Madison said to her, "I'll give you an engagement ring. I don't have much money so it'll probably have a small diamond with a flaw."

"I have an idea," Rho said. "I don't want you to spend too much, so why don't we go to a pawn shop and look for a ring there. I don't mind if someone else has worn it before me."

"I've never been to a pawn shop," Madison said, raising his eyebrows.

"Me neither, but there will be many rings to choose from and checking out the situation ought to be interesting."

Snow was floating down from a gray sky when Rho and Madison entered the Crown Pawn Shop. It featured guitars, typewriters, and record collections. A clerk who wore a toupee that was askew approached them. "We're looking for an engagement ring," Madison said, as he tightly held on to Rho's hand.

The clerk guided them to a glass showcase. Rho tried on some rings that were too large and some that were too small. "Here's an unusual antique ring," the clerk said.

Rho smiled. "May I please try it on?"

The ring proved to be a perfect fit. It was gold with one diamond in a centered triangle resting on a larger triangle. Leaves were encrusted with 18 shiny diamonds. Rho's eyes shone with pleasure.

"If you buy this ring now," the clerk said, "I'll deduct ten per cent."

"What do you think?" Madison asked, taking out his wallet.

"It's beautiful. I love it, thank you."

On Rho's birthday the couple returned to the same pawn shop. This time Madison bought Rho a pearl necklace. The next trip to the pawn shop was on their first anniversary and he bought her a gold bracelet. Soon after that Madison enrolled in a two-year program at a technical school and graduated with honors. He learned enough to open his own business. He prospered so much that they were able to buy a home on five acres of land.

When Rho gave birth to a 7 lb. 6 oz. son, Madison bought Rho diamond earrings from the same pawn shop. They named the son Andrew.

Two years later Rho gave birth to Jessica, and Madison showed up at the hospital with a thick gold necklace that he got from 'their' pawn shop and with a large jewelry box that he bought in Macy's. Rho showed her sister-in-law Denise all her precious jewelry, and her sister-in-law dragged *her* husband to the Crown Pawn shop. Denise never revealed to her friends how her husband had been able to afford all the diamond pieces he continued to buy there.

When Rho encouraged her father to buy jewelry for her mother, her father agreed but her mother demurred, "I don't like jewelry. I'd rather wear scarves around my neck."

Her loss for sure.

When Jessica and Andrew were old enough to go to intermediate school, Rho joined the PTA. She willingly shared her privileged information with the women she became friendly with. They all frequented the Crown Pawn shop like bees in a flower garden. The time came when Andrew was an adult and had chosen a young woman to marry. "Tell her you can get a good bargain for an engagement ring at *my* pawn shop," Rho advised her son. The girl was a snob, scoffed at the idea, and broke off the engagement. Andrew never listened to his mother again about pawn-shop shopping.

Jessica had the opposite result. Her fiancé was thrilled when he saved thousands of dollars on an engagement ring for her.

As their business expanded due to the many recommendations by Rho and Madison, the Crown Pawn Shop bought the stores on either side of it, added upper stories on top of them, and opened a mid-size department store. The manager was so thrilled with Rho and Madison that he sent them birthday and anniversary cards and gave them huge discounts.

When Jessica gave birth to her twin boys, she was blessed not only with healthy babies but gifts of a ruby and diamond necklace from the pawn-shop owner.

Time marches on and after 20 years a now-white-haired Rho had accumulated tons of precious jewelry. She collected treasures the way Madison collected stamps. Madison installed a safe in their bedroom to protect Rho's collection.

At their 50th-anniversary gala Madison, with a champagne flute in his liver-spotted hand, rose to his feet and addressed the 250 assembled guests. "My dear family and friends, I offer an unusual toast to the owner and the manager of the Crown Pawn Shop. 51 years ago Rho and I entered a small shop and I bought Rho the engagement ring she still wears to this very day. It started as a habit and turned into a tradition that on birthdays and anniversaries we shopped for fine jewelry at the same pawn shop. We spread the word around about how pleased we were with the shop and more and more people patronized it. On my son Andrew's birthdays I bought him the watches he admired, and on my daughter Jessica's birthdays I gave her the necklaces she cherished. My darling wife always selected something lovely from the growing amounts of jewelry the shop featured. Many of our friends here have followed the tradition we created. And so the business has thrived beyond anyone's wildest dreams. The store provided win-win solutions for the problems of what to buy for loved ones.

"When I met Rho, I was a poor struggling fellow with no prospects. I couldn't even get the words out when I proposed. As I matured, I attended a technical school and afterwards started my own business. It became successful. I really don't expect that *my* customers will invite Rho and me to their anniversary parties as we have invited the owner and manager of the Crown Pawn Shop to ours. Now gentlemen, please stand up and take a bow."

The men in their tuxedos stood as the audience recognized them and clapped hands very enthusiastically.

"I hope that all of you who are here tonight will continue our tradition."

The applause which followed was deafening.

How Has the Pandemic Affected Me?
(submitted to pandemic@palmango.com)

My title is interrogative, because, as the question in the call is multi-faceted–How has Covid-19 pandemic affected your life and your thoughts about the future, life in general, and the world?–my response is far-ranging, multi-leveled, changeable, and even self-contradictory. Since an essay requires the imposition of logical order, however, I proceed from (shocking and unabashedly, but honest) self-centered considerations to stoic ones to subjective religious understandings. The latter requires clarification at the outset. A believing Jew/Judaist, I have traversed more versions of Jewish religion and culture than many people know exist; but I also have universalist strivings, having taught Religion for eight years at a Catholic university (Villanova) and having been the Latin teacher for a subsequent eight years in the two diocesan high schools of South Bend and Mishawaka, Indiana.

My self-centered considerations involve guilt, but perhaps not as much as they should. For my wife Reva and I are deriving benefit from the new "social distancing" rules. We actually enjoy staying at home more. We have no communal obligations, such as our weekly writing-club meeting. We play many more Scrabble games than before. We take longer naps. And we are writing more. A serious pitfall for me in the situation, to be sure, is that my diet has gotten "shot to hell." After having lost 25 pounds by the end of 2019, I fear I put back 35 in the month of April 2020 alone. It is not a consolation that the gain in my midriff's volume is inversely proportional to the decrease of my desk's piles and piles of papers because of my more disciplined "de-cluttering" in the greater amount of free time that I now have.

Other benefits are economic. We each have gotten stimulus money, though our writing "businesses" are not suffering financially. Any more than usual, that is. And our expenses have lessened. We don't go to restaurants. And with our staying at home more our vehicles consume far less gas than before.

Tempering these complacent reflections of personal benefit is the recognition that my wife and I in South Florida–and our children, grandchildren, great-grandchildren, and my brother and sister-in-law in or near the metropolitan areas of New York City, Philadelphia, Chicago, and Jerusalem–can catch the disease at any time and even be felled by it.

Complacent thoughts give way to stoic ones, which involve skeptical resistance to ideas of the virus's having a "higher purpose," objectively speaking–for example, a reaction to human indifference to global warming, or overpopulation, or wealth inequality, or xenophobia and other kinds of moral hubris. I incline towards accepting the scientific judgment that a biological organism such as a virus has a single overriding purpose–to reproduce. Its spread owes its need to find more and more lungs in which it can procreate, mutating as much as it has to in the process, just so its species will not die out. For once it can no longer reproduce that is what must happen. The obvious does not even need to be stated. We practice "social distancing" to deny the virus fertile "spreading places." And if wayward germs do somehow penetrate the gates of our condo community–as has happened, resulting in the deaths of a small number of people–well, *c'est la mort!* (That's the death!). At least they only zapped a few of us here.

Instead of my ironic French exclamation, I was about to write, "But for the Grace of God go I." I caught myself, realizing that would be a contradiction of my emphasis of disbelief in the disease's having a higher purpose. I, analogously, don't believe that the Holocaust was the supernatural punishment of God for the sins of the Jewish people or a prerequisite provided by God to motivate the United Nations to create the State of Israel, the reestablishment of the Jewish Commonwealth of old.

Here, however, is where religious understandings, subjective ones, are vitally important. Plagues have occurred throughout human history. They decimated the Israelites in the Sinai desert, not just the Egyptians in Egypt. The Talmud relates the deaths from a plague of 24,000 students of Rabbi Aqiva in the years of the Bar Kokhva Revolt (132-135); and whereas there is a scholarly interpretation that many of them actually were killed in the fight against the Romans, a large number of them, if the interpretation is correct, may have been infected by the plague as well. Shakespeare knew of plagues, as is vividly attested in *King Lear*.

As we fight this contagion, I write this with much emotion, our need is to bring our own meaning to our lives–as individuals, in our families, in our communities, in our cities, and in our nations. We need to be as united as possible in pooling our resources and in supporting both our medical specialists and caregivers on the front lines and the recuperating victims and their families as the pandemic runs its course.

I mentioned the Holocaust earlier. Having been born in 1942 in Boston, I escaped the Holocaust only because my paternal and maternal grandparents had emigrated to America at the turn of the 20th century from Kovno (Kaunas), Lithuania, and from Slavuta in the Ukraine, respectively. Thinking about surviving in the death camps has been ingrained in my consciousness since my earliest youth. A cousin I recently reconnected with revealed to me that she is alienated from religion because of the Holocaust. In expressing my own point of view to her, including the emphasis that no one should self-righteously presume to understand a supernatural rationale for it, the need is for people to embody the best possible moral behavior in the face of what appears to be evil, human as well as natural.

Namely, a starving concentration camp inmate who shared a portion of meager rations with another in the hope that the other would have a chance of surviving was a far more commendable human being than the one who didn't and left the other to fend for self in hopelessness.

Who Says We're Not What We Say We Are?

by Allan Korn and Eddie Levenson

[Allan's turn first.] I am a salesperson at heart who has mastered the art and skill of convincing customers to part with their money. In my verbal communication I utilize proven outer- and inner-directed techniques. I learned quickly that the most common mistake of a salesperson is talking too much. True conviction is conveyed not with more words but fewer. Lincoln's Gettysburg Address, for example, contains 267 words; the Ten Commandments, 163. Saying less but communicating more, while employing strategic silence, has been my key to success.

How could I change from using sparse words verbally to becoming a multi-written-words author? I stared at my blank computer screen for what seemed to be an eternity and decided to write about a real event. I showed the draft to my wife Ellen, a retired English teacher. Her critique was scathing. "Your punctuation is atrocious. You mix up tenses. Other errors of yours are unspeakable. You have no dialogue. The piece is a total mess. You must rewrite it."

[Eddie's note. Our wives, Ellen and Reva, are "the loves of our lives." But, in the immortal words of Joe E. Brown at the conclusion of *Some Like It Hot*, "Nobody's perfect!"]

Our daughter Rachel also had something to say, "Dad, what is this? You can't say this. Just describe things. Listen to what Mom said. And don't show this to me again!"

[Eddie's second note. Not even daughters.][1]

Nothing, however, was said about the content. I decided that writing is telling a story as best as one can for the reader's enjoyment. I'll leave the editing of grammar and punctuation to the experts. Repeating to myself "I am a writer! I am a writer!" I steeled myself to ignore my wife's and daughter's severe criticisms. It is my own opinion of my writing that is the one that counts. Feeling this way, I produced each of the four last pieces of mine in this anthology [*The View From Kings Point,* 2020] more fluently than the respective preceding one; and each, I felt, was progressively more interesting to me. Writing has become enjoyable and rewarding. I've become expansive in my written self-expression. I have become a writer!

[Second, Eddie's turn.] Whereas my new friend and colleague Allan has mastered the art and skill of precision and concision, I, though paying lip service to those ideals, sin greatly on the side of excessive verbosity and don't really expect that I will ever be cured of that. I'm fortunate not to be in sales. What I, however, wish for more than anything in the world, I often think, is for my sense of humor to be praised, or at least acknowledged. I crave compliments when I say something funny and don't ever seem to get as many for doing so as I would like.

My insecurity about ambivalence re my humor stemmed from the "barely grudging acceptance" it received on the part of my father, William Julius Levenson of blessed memory––or so he pretended–– when I was growing up. He was the champion wit in the family, not I. After ironic *double entendres* of mine Dad used to narrow his

---

[1] *Note to the two "Eddie notes" above. I mean this note to be a *volta* (an ironic turn in the manner of the concluding couplet of a Shakespearean sonnet). Yes, humor is important, but it can be oversought and overdone; and Allan and I may well be guilty of that. Somewhat, at least. In making wife Ellen and daughter Rachel "exaggerated comic foils," we, in a way, exemplified the foolishness excoriated so repeatedly in the Book of Ecclesiastes that "Vanity of vanities, all is vanity"; for Ellen and Rachel had, of course, benevolent intentions and constructive purpose.

eyes, shrug his shoulders, and look over at my brother Rob, who was doing the same. Both, then, simultaneously used to utter the words, in mock disassociation, "Edward's humor." I titled my first multi-genres collection, which included a "Humor" section, *"Edward's Humor" and More* as if to appeal retrospectively to my Dad Heavenward, "See, Dad, some people down here do think I'm funny."

This anthology has taken a year to come to fruition. I have put together a different kind of collection–forthcoming shortly, God willing—in a fraction of that time. It is *Edward's Xlibris Best*, and it has a "Humor" section, as did my first book. When readers would have a glimpse at that section in particular, I pray they would not forget to laugh.

Of my four children, my youngest, Ben, it has seemed, gets the most embarrassed by my funny stories. Maybe, I should admit, it's because I regale total strangers with them on our way out of restaurants when he is in a hurry and since he has heard the same stories a number of times previously.

Sensing Ben needed an infusion of cash for his recent June vacation in North Carolina, I mailed him a check and gave him a heads-up about it on Facebook Messenger, "Ben, Santa Claus will be coming down the chimney early this year with something for you."

Pausing about seven seconds, I messaged again, "Ben, if the house where you're staying doesn't have a chimney, I hope the owner has Homeowner's Insurance."

Pausing another seven seconds, I added my signature question, "Ben, WHO SAYS I'M NOT FUNNY?"

This time Ben replied with unprecedented praise, "Hahaha! *Abba* (Dad, in Hebrew). That was *really* very funny!"

Moved almost to tears, I needed a few extra seconds to compose myself and I messaged my response, "Ben, you've just made me the happiest *Abba* in the world!"